POETRY AND THE FOUNTAIN OF LIGHT

POETRY AND THE
FOUNTAIN OF LIGHT

*Observations on the Conflict between
Christian and Classical Traditions
in Seventeenth-Century Poetry*

H. R. SWARDSON
Ohio University

UNIVERSITY OF MISSOURI PRESS

COLUMBIA

PRINTED IN GREAT BRITAIN
in 12 point Bembo type
BY SIMSON SHAND LTD
LONDON, HERTFORD AND HARLOW

ACKNOWLEDGMENT

I am happy to be able to acknowledge the extent of the debt I owe in this book to the man to whom it is dedicated, Leonard Unger. He suggested the study to me in the beginning and envisioned its proper outcome from the earliest stages; in our every discussion he has been unhesitatingly free with his own insights and unfailingly kind in his guidance of mine. If the work has fallen short, or strayed from its first prospects, it is no fault of his.

To my wife, who joins me in this dedication, I would like, among those things that can be recognized here, to speak my gratitude for her good sense as a critic and for her practical contribution to scholarship's material needs. Without her help this book would not have been written.

CONTENTS

Introduction
The Fountain of Light

THERE ARE many ways of looking at the cultural and intellectual revolution that takes place in England in the seventeenth century. It is a period which, in the twentieth century, has inspired a variety of explanatory formulas. One reason for this, apparently, is the feeling among moderns that in explaining what happened in the seventeenth century they are also explaining their own condition. It is felt that the period of conflict between medieval and modern habits of mind illuminates, in a peculiarly critical light, the nature and problems of the modern world; that the great turn toward secularism in Western civilization that set us on our present track was cornered most sharply here in England in these years, and that this is consequently a dramatic and instructive moment in the history of ideas. Modern thinkers find themselves in sympathy with the minds that felt the pressures of this turn most acutely, particularly with those minds which, like Sir Thomas Browne, seemed to keep their balance under such pressures. Those who find a loss of equilibrium in their own century feel a kinship with and admiration for such minds. Undoubtedly the appeal that seventeenth-century poetry has had in modern times has derived in part from an admiration for a certain kind of sensibility, which is believed to have prevailed at this time more than at any other. Formulas of varying complexity have dealt with this phenomenon; some formulas, like T. S. Eliot's 'dissociation of sensibility', taking departure from the special character of the seventeenth-century setting and sensibility, have been expanded into whole theories of literary history and aesthetics.

13

As is true for any age, the formula or perspective we adopt, the terms in which we conceive the setting, affects our reading of the poetry. For the literary critic some terms are more useful than others, or they are useful in different ways. The way to determine this usefulness, I take it, is to adopt the perspective provided by one's chosen terms and see what kind of insight into the poetry this perspective allows. What I propose to do here is to explore a perspective in just this way. I am not primarily interested in making a new formula, or in developing a theory in the history of ideas, but in analysing and evaluating certain seventeenth-century poems in the most revealing light. To do this I will make use of a perspective, or formula, but it is not a new one. It is obvious and familiar and old-fashioned, but it has not yet, I think, been fully exploited for critical purposes in the study of seventeenth-century poetry.

The nature and worth of this perspective is probably best revealed as we go along, rather than stated abstractly here at the beginning. My intention is to view the central fact of the seventeenth-century literary climate, the conflict familiar in all the books on the Renaissance, in the familiar terms of a conflict between Christian and classical traditions, interpreting these terms more strictly and literally, however, than is customary. But there is obviously more to such a view than a bald statement can do justice to. The best way to go about constructing our perspective is to take one poem that will reveal the main issues clearly and give us some concrete terms to work with. A poem by Thomas Carew, *To . . . George Sandys, On his Translation of the Psalms*, will serve. It is a poem very useful to the student of seventeenth-century literature, and one particularly suited to introduce the subject of this book:

> I press not to the choir, nor dare I greet
> The holy place with my unhallow'd feet;
> My unwash'd Muse pollutes not things divine,
> Nor mingles her profaner notes with thine;
> Here humbly at the porch she list'ning stays,
> And with glad ears sucks in thy sacred lays.
> So devout penitents of old were wont,

14

Some without door and some beneath the font,
To stand and hear the Church's liturgies,
Yet not assist the solemn exercise.
Sufficeth her that she a lay-place gain,
To trim thy vestments, or but bear thy train;
Though nor in tune nor wing she reach thy lark,
Her lyric feet may dance before the Ark.
Who knows but that her wand'ring eyes, that run
Now hunting glow-worms, may adore the sun?
A pure flame may, shot by Almighty Power
Into my breast, the earthy flame devour;
My eyes in penitential dew may steep
That brine which they for sensual love did weep:
So though 'gainst Nature's course, fire may be quench'd
With fire, and water be with water drench'd.
Perhaps my restless soul, tir'd with pursuit
Of mortal beauty, seeking without fruit
Contentment there, which hath not, when enjoy'd
Quench'd all her thirst, nor satisfi'd, though cloy'd,
Weary of her vain search below, above
In the first fair may find th' immortal love.
Prompted by thy example then, no more
In moulds of clay will I my God adore;
But tear those idols from my heart, and write
What his blest Sp'rit, not fond love, shall indite.
Then I no more shall court the verdant bay,
But the dry leafless trunk on Golgotha,
And rather strive to gain from thence one thorn
Than all the flourishing wreaths by laureates worn.[1]

Here, we recognize at once, is the characteristic posture of the secular love poet reminded of his place in Christian society. The position, with all its discomfort, is a familiar one in English poetry before Dryden, and not hard to understand. We think of the long tradition of retraction and palinode peculiar to the literature of Christian countries, and know that this is in the same spirit, and has the same ultimate source, as those periodic laments by medieval and Renaissance poets repenting their service to love and the secular muse. The characteristic note of these laments is Sidney's

splendidis longum valedico nugis—a long farewell to glittering trifles
—and, though there are many ways of phrasing it, the tone is
much the same. Carew's poem reminds us of more famous examples of the love poet's turnabout: Spenser's penitent hymns to
heavenly love and beauty, Vaughan's firm repudiation of his
'lascivious fictions', Chaucer's epilogue to the *Troilus* and his retraction at the end of the *Canterbury Tales*. For a motto for the
whole tradition we might perhaps call to mind, appropriately
enough, Petrarch's 'I' vo piangendo i miei passati tempi/ I quai
posi in amar cosa mortale'—I go lamenting my past history that
I spent in the love of mortal things.[2]

This is the broadest tradition in which Carew's poem belongs,
the tradition of recantation and repentance. From one point of
view, it is not worth much discussion as a tradition. What we
are dealing with here, it might be said, is merely a cropping up of
the familiar contempt of the world, the otherworldly spirit. The
recantation by the 'worldly' poet, we might say, is essentially
nothing more than a renunciation of the 'false worldes brotelnosse'
according to the time-honoured demands of the Christian *ascesis*.
This phenomenon, far broader than poetry, needs no explanation
to the Christian mind. Nor, being so broad, is it particularly
interesting for critical purposes. It is as easy to sin in verse as it is
any other way, and repentance in poetry may be too universally
human to be worth separating as a literary tradition.

True enough, a poet, as a person, may sin like any other man;
one can think carnal thoughts, or speak them, or act them out, as
well as put them in a poem, and the poetry may be incidental to
the vice. This source of a poet's discomfort is, admittedly, not very
distinctive. True also that extra-literary sins, from the literary
historian's point of view, may not be very interesting. What *is*
interesting, of course, what makes the tradition and Carew's poem
worth special attention, is the sin that attaches to the literary
activity itself, the offence peculiar to the poet's practice as a poet and
the tradition he works in. Discomfort on this score is apparently
the real source of our interest in these poems as a class. Mixed as it
is with the other kind of discomfort, it should, at the beginning,
be clearly distinguished as the proper object of our attention.

When we have done this we find ourselves face to face with that ancient and profound conflict between secular letters and the Christian faith that lies in the background of all European literature. For the historian this is a broad and complicated phenomenon. For the present purpose, to understand the springs of Carew's discomfort, we may glance briefly at the essential features of this conflict. It is, first of all, a conflict generated by attitudes timelessly and characteristically Christian, not special or limited, but central to a Christian way of looking at things. Sir Herbert Grierson, observing that this conflict reaches a peak of intensity in the seventeenth century, calls attention to a nineteenth-century writer, John Foster, to illustrate its pervasiveness in Western culture. Foster, in an essay titled 'On the Aversion of Men of Taste to Evangelical Religion', reveals very clearly some of the attitudes that underlie this conflict. He asserts that

> what is denominated Polite Literature . . . is, for the greater part, hostile to the religion of Christ; partly by introducing insensibly a certain order of opinions unconsonant, or at least not identical, with the principles of that religion; and still more, by training the feelings to a habit alien from its spirit. And in this assertion I do not refer to writers palpably irreligious, who have laboured and intended to seduce the passions into vice, or the judgment into the rejection of Divine truth; but to the general community of those elegant and ingenious authors who are read and admired by the Christian world, held essential to a liberal education, and to the progressive accomplishment of the mind in subsequent life, and studied often without an apprehension, or even a thought, of their injuring the views and temper of spirits advancing, with the New Testament for their chief guide, into another world.[3]

A complaint like this, which could, in effect, be a voice from almost any Christian century, is a useful reminder of the broad basis of the Christian challenge to belles lettres and shows us the largest setting in which to put Carew's poem.

We recognize in this challenge the same otherworldliness that rebukes and discomposes the man as well as the poet. 'My kingdom is not of this world,' said Jesus (*John*, 18:36), and the texts supporting the Christian *ascesis* are familiar ones: Love not the world, neither the things that are in the world. If any man love the world, the love of the father is not in him (*I John*, 2:15). He that loveth his life shall lose it; and he that hateth his life in this world shall keep it unto life eternal (*John*, 12:25). Obviously much of the Christian conflict with poetry can simply be regarded as a continuing skirmish in that old war against the world, the flesh, and the devil. Insofar as poetry traffics in the world, insofar as the stuff of poems is the sensuous stuff of worldly experience, poetry is in danger of the judgment. Christian otherworldliness may work on poetry more subtly than this, as we shall observe, but this is its obvious and immediate operation.

Next in Foster's remarks we recognize an element perhaps even more significant in its effect on secular poetry. We see that what confronts poetry here, in addition to (or superimposed on) the broader otherworldly tendencies, is nothing less than the fundamental spirit of exclusiveness peculiar to Christianity. The Judeo-Christian religion, as everyone knows, is distinguished among religions by the demand it makes for an exclusive commitment, a demand that not only excludes other religious allegiances, but, followed rigidly, tends to exclude all interests not contributary to the soul's end. It is the demand of *Matthew*, 22:37, the first and great commandment, read in its strictest sense: Thou shalt love the Lord thy God with all thy heart, and with all thy soul, and with all thy mind. This spirit of exclusiveness, Hebraic in origin, permeates Christian culture and, in conjunction with the otherworldly spirit, underlies the Christian protest against secular art and literature from the beginning of the Christian era.

It has two dimensions. The first pertains to the goal of life in general; it is seen in the belief that man's exclusive real concern on earth is the health of his soul. Whatever does not contribute to the soul's salvation is a distraction, 'vain' and 'idle'—to use the usual Puritan and Patristic epithets. More activities than secular poetry, certainly, have come under the ban of this sort of exclusiveness. The second pertains more particularly to writing. It is seen in the characteristic insistence that Christian writing provides an exclusive revelation of the way, the truth, and the life. This claim renders suspect all writing outside the faith, particularly forcing an antagonism toward pagan classical writing. Both aspects of the spirit of exclusiveness are seen in the vision of 'spirits advancing, with the New Testament for their chief guide, into another world'.

Clearly this spirit is not restricted to particular sects or to extremes of zeal, though, where it affects poetry, we are accustomed to take all our examples from the Puritans. But even those who most vigorously defend poetry against the Puritan attack recognize and accept the logical consequences for poetry of these paramount claims. 'I cannot denie', wrote Sir John Harington, an urbane man of letters, in 1591, 'but to us that are Christians, in respect of the high end of all, which is the health of our soules, not only Poetrie but all other studies of Philosophy are in a manner vaine and superfluous, yea (as the wise man saith) whatsoever is under the sunne is vanitie of vanities, and nothing but vanitie.'[4]

If, in remarking the spirit of exclusiveness at the bottom of the Christian reaction to poetry, we are not down to bedrock, we at least lay hold of an attitude that, operating with certain otherworldly conceptions, is sufficient cause and sustenance of the hostility toward poetry. Given the Christian attitude toward the soul's health, and toward the literature that alone may minister to it, the deprecation of secular imaginative literature would seem to follow naturally. Certainly, remembering this trait in Christianity, we can understand how 'idleness' and 'fruitlessness' can readily be charged against poetry, as against other pleasurable distractions of the mind; or, if not 'charged', how consciousness of such a challenge, so unanswerable, could discomfit even a careless Christian who gives himself to matter 'vaine and superfluous' and to feelings 'alien' from the spirit of a religion that admits no compromise.

If Carew's poem is useful to us in showing the general posture of discomfort taken by the love poet in Christian surroundings, a phenomenon not peculiar to the seventeenth century, it is also useful in showing the pitch of this discomfort in the seventeenth century; it may serve as an index of the strength of this feeling, and an indication of its form, in the period we are to deal with. Certainly from the other kinds of evidence that reveal the temper of an age we might expect the self-consciousness and guilt of the 'carnal' poet to be at a peak of intensity at this time. In the immediate background we think not only of the Puritan-led agitation against the arts but of the whole 're-awakened temper of early Christianity, other-worldly, intransigent in its attitude towards any acceptance of the world as an end in itself, as something to be enjoyed'[5]—that is, the spirit of the Reformation. We think of the great agitation, among the poets and the pious alike, to turn poetry to Christian subjects, and of the great popularity of Du Bartas and Wither, explainable now only on the grounds that they seemed to satisfy this demand. In no other age, certainly, do we get such a consistent pattern for the poet's career: youthful carnal poems, classical imitations, then repentance, followed by religious poems, hymns, psalm translations. We may also remember that, in prose, parallel to the secular poet's occasional defensive posture in his poetry, runs the primary effort of Renaissance literary criticism, the defence of imaginative literature on theoretical grounds. This task, we understand, is forced on men of letters like Sidney by the revival of belles lettres amidst the undispelled Christian suspicion of literary art descending through medieval traditions. In the late sixteenth and early seventeenth centuries we recognize an intensification of the kind of religious feeling (of which Puritanism is only one manifestation) that makes trouble for poetry—the otherworldly spirit—at the same time that poets are mastering and realizing the full possibilities of the classical forms. The result is a deepening of a natural antipathy. All this should prepare us to recognize how Carew's poem reflects the important pressures that bear on a poet in his age, as perhaps a greater poem would not, and that we are justified in taking it as representative.

In the poem's more immediate surroundings we may observe that the early seventeenth century is full of poems by love poets hailing, with particular fervour, this or that poet's translation or paraphrase of the psalms. Nothing is more highly praised than poetry turned to a religious subject. Most love poets themselves turned, usually late in life, to 'pious pieces', and psalm versification was a popular activity in both this and the preceding century—as witness the names of Wyatt, Surrey, Gascoigne, Sidney, Donne, Carew, Denham, Henry King, Wither, and Milton among those who turned their hands to it. Though the pious poems are consistently overvalued artistically, the comment on them gives us a nice insight into the poet's conception of his calling at this time. The first thing we notice about Carew's poem is his consciousness, from his place in the secular literary tradition, of an unsanctioned calling, making him unworthy to approach the holy place with 'unhallow'd feet'. Herrick felt the same way about his 'unbaptized Rhimes', which stood before God 'uncircumsis'd, unseason'd, and prophane', still shut out by Hebraic exclusiveness. Carew's reference to his 'unwash'd Muse' most clearly reveals the whole conception. The secular muse is 'unwashed' in the sense that it is unbaptized, still in the pagan literary tradition; and also in the sense that it is plain dirty, smirched with the world and its impurities. The term reminds us how much each seventeenth-century poet really possessed two muses which, following Carew's own image, we might call the clean one and the dirty one. A study of the essential features of seventeenth-century poetry might indeed very appropriately be titled 'The Two Muses'. There was no doubt that the dirty one, whose lineage was suspect and who, in the poets who worried about her, usually inspired the best poetry, could receive no official sanction. As Carew's poem indicates, the best that could be said (and this was said often) was that the profane muse, being highly skilled in art, might act as handmaid to the divine muse, whose worth and superiority rested mainly in one supreme possession, truth. Thus skill in art may adorn Christian truth—if adornment be entirely proper. But even this, as remains to be seen, was a ticklish question.

The reform of the love poet's muse is presented by Carew in a series of conventional contrasts that demonstrate her position in the Christian scheme of values. Eyes that may adore the sun (as usual, the Son) are employed seeking glow-worms—the fault the Puritans attacked under the heading 'idleness'. The poet's reform is seen as the transformation of the fire of lust into the fire of zeal, the common contrast of earthly and heavenly love: 'A pure flame

may, shot by Almighty Power/ Into my breast, the earthy flame
devour.' And the tears of repentance are set against the lover's
tears: 'My eyes in penitential dew may steep/ That brine which
they for sensual love did weep.' It is a common image, most
familiar in Donne:

> O might those sighes and teares returne againe
> Into my breast and eyes, which I have spent,
> That I might in this holy discontent
> Mourne with some fruit, as I have mourn'd in vaine.[6]

The next to last contrast sets the immortal love and beauty of
Christ, the 'first fair', against the usual object of love poetry, the
woman. All these contrasts are frequent in the religious poet's
deprecation of love poetry, and also in the love poet's repentance.
We note them to establish the conventional nature, the representa-
tiveness, of Carew's sentiments.

The concluding images, still conventional, are the ones I would
most like to dwell on, however. They seem to condense the whole
series of contrasts the poem has been making:

> Then I no more shall court the verdant bay,
> But the dry, leafless trunk on Golgotha,
> And rather strive to gain from thence one thorn,
> Than all the flourishing wreaths by laureates worn.

Here the 'verdant bay' stands for the classical line, pagan, sensuous,
luxuriant, of nature, rich for poetry, yet trivial and false; the
austere 'trunk on Golgotha' stands for the bare and valuable 'truth'
opposed to this, Christ's truth 'clad with simplenesse' as Herbert
calls it. The contrast of crowns, the crown of thorns against the
laureate crown, repeats and condenses the same antithesis in an
image we shall meet frequently. How natural and appropriate it is
to cast the whole conflict into these terms, and figure the opposed
values as a classical-Christian opposition. Carew's closing lines
remind us properly how all the weight of suspicion and dis-
approval naturally focuses on the classicism of the secular literary
tradition. From religious and literary history we know, of course,

that these have been the clearest and most dramatic terms in which the whole conflict with imaginative literature has presented itself to the imagination. Since, for all practical purposes, the literary tradition *is* the classical tradition, speaking of a classical-Christian conflict is a way of speaking, in perhaps the most convenient terms, of that larger and vaguer conflict discussed above. The deeper issues can't help shining through these immediate terms—which, in turn, to change the metaphor, give us a handle by which to grasp an otherwise rather amorphous subject. There is no doubt, as Carew's poem shows, that this way of looking at the issue has provided the most appropriate and richly dramatic imagery for the poets. It certainly points to that aspect of Christianity's old quarrel with poetry that is most interesting for critical purposes.

What the classical stands for and how it fits into this conflict may be reviewed quickly. We know that there has existed, from the beginnings of Western civilization, a sense of opposition between the classical and the Christian. We know, to repeat, that the responsibility for this feeling lies in the character of the Christian religion, specifically its insistence on an exclusive revelation of the truth and the light—the characteristic Hebraic exclusiveness that casts suspicion on all writing outside the faith and particularly rejects classical pagan works, which, by their intrinsic qualities, seem naturally antithetic to Christian values anyway. Yet, the attraction of the classical has been undeniable and continuous. Even those who, in the days of the early church, felt the Hebraic exclusiveness most strongly, felt also the great attraction of the classical authors. It is this simultaneous attraction and repulsion that would let us speak of a tension between the two traditions in any particular writer.

A classic early example of this tension, from a psychological view, is St Jerome's famous anti-Ciceronian vision. He describes it in a letter:

But even when I was on my way to Jerusalem to fight the good fight there, I could not bring myself to forgo the library which with great care and labor I had got together at Rome. And so, miserable man that I was, I would fast, only to read Cicero afterwards. I would spend many nights in vigil, I would shed bitter tears called from my inmost heart by the remembrance of my past sins; and then I would take up Plautus again. Whenever I returned to my right senses and began to read the prophets, their language seemed harsh and barbarous.[7]

Then, during a fever, Jerome has a vision in which he is dragged before the judgment seat: 'I was asked to state my condition and replied that I was a Christian. But he who presided said: "Thou liest; thou art a Ciceronian, not a Christian. 'For where thy treasure is there will thy heart be also.' " ' Jerome is then scourged, and begs pardon under penalty of 'the extreme of torture' if 'ever I read again the works of Gentile authors ... if ever again I possess worldly books'. He then returns to the world to read 'books of God' with greater zeal than he ever read the 'books of men'.

There were, of course, ways of circumventing this exclusiveness, and the strategies adopted are testimony both to the strength of the exclusive doctrine and to the power of the urge to find legal loopholes. The pattern for reconciliation is set early through the attempts, by both Jews and early Christian writers, to accommodate discordant material within the faith itself. An example of this is Augustine's allegorizing of the otherwise embarrassing *Song of Songs*. It is a strategy that permits Christians, faced with the necessity to give profane material a sacred meaning, to re-interpret pagan writing, allegorizing Virgil, moralizing Ovid, etc., imposing a Christian colour on the classical authors which, as St Jerome felt, were so hard to abandon. Where this is not possible, the classical material remains under suspicion and, even in a blameless context, is likely to be treated with some uneasiness by Christian poets.

If we are going to speak of a classical-Christian tension in the seventeenth century, meaning by this expression what St Jerome felt, we need go no further than Milton to illustrate and justify our terms. I refer to the famous rejection by Christ in *Paradise Regained*[8] of all the learning and art of the classical world offered to Him by Satan in the second temptation. 'All knowledge is not couch't in Moses Law,/The Pentateuch or what the Prophets wrote,' says Satan, displaying Greece and the city Milton revered, 'built nobly, pure the air, and light the soil,/Athens the eye of Greece, Mother of Arts/And Eloquence, native to famous wits.' Then, with all the art and learning of the classical world in view, he offers all to the Saviour, who replies,

> Think not but that I know these things, or think
> I know them not; not therefore am I short
> Of knowing what I ought: he who receives
> Light from above, from the fountain of light,
> No other doctrine needs, though granted true.

Jesus then rejects the philosophers, who are ignorant of God, and after them the poets, who are charged with all the familiar complaints:

> Or if I would delight my private hours
> With Music or with Poem, where so soon
> As in our native Language can I find
> That solace? All our Law and Story strew'd
> With Hymns, our Psalms with artful terms inscrib'd,
> Our Hebrew Songs and Harps in Babylon,
> That pleas'd so well our Victors ear, declare
> That rather Greece from us these arts deriv'd;
> Ill imitated, while they loudest sing
> The vices of thir Deities, and thir own
> In Fable, Hymn, or Song, so personating
> Thir gods ridiculous, and themselves past shame.
> Remove their swelling Epithetes thick laid
> As varnish on a Harlot's cheek, the rest,
> Thin sown with aught of profit or delight,
> Will far be found unworthy to compare
> With Sion's songs, to all true tasts excelling,
> Where God is prais'd aright, and Godlike men,
> The Holiest of Holies, and his Saints.

We see in the passage the final victory in Milton, after what life-long opposition, of the Hebraic over the Hellenic, and recognize the same exclusiveness of the Hebraic kind of truth, the necessarily single and unrivalled fountain of light, that moved the Church Fathers.

All this is familiar ground. In a way, the tension between classical and Christian traditions is the most obvious fact in the field of seventeenth-century literature. The case for the presence and influence of the tension hardly needs to be argued. It is the kind of obvious issue that requires us to be on our guard more against truisms and commonplaces than against over-subtle insights. If there is any cause for wonder it should be that this fact, or formula, is not kept more in the foreground and applied more systematically than it has been to the reading of seventeenth-century poetry. It is partly, perhaps, this very familiarity that calls for a careful understanding of terms here. We want to give an expression like 'tension between classical and Christian traditions' the necessary historical significance, yet we really do not want to claim more for it than an agreement upon and ordering of the obvious.

As for the individual terms, I am sure it will be understood how much the meaning of the term 'Christian tradition' is limited by the present context. What we have in view when we use the term is primarily those key habits of mind described above as 'other-worldliness' and 'exclusiveness'. The attitudes covered by the term within this context, the context of poetry's difficulties, are not all of the Christian tradition, of course, but merely lie within the range of attitudes called Christian. Certainly nothing here is to be taken as a general characterization of Christianity and its influence, or as an assessment of its essential beliefs, or even as an evaluation of its total effect on literature. The Christian religion as a great source of inspiration to art and literature in its own way is simply something I am not concerned with here. The kind of piety treated here, the kind that generates the conflict that concerns us, is obviously not all of Christianity, and we could argue its relative position and importance in Christianity endlessly according to our varying conceptions of what is *really* Christian. All that I mean to say here is that this kind of piety lies prominently within the area called Christian, that it is obviously important in Christian history, and that it has certain demonstrable consequences for secular poetry.

It should be clear that more lies behind these terms 'otherworldliness' and 'exclusiveness' than we can do justice to here. We cannot rest in them, however, without at least a glance at what they hide. For one thing, the effect of Christian otherworldliness is more profound than that revealed in the familiar moral fight against world, flesh, and devil. Deeper in the background, and harder to fix, is a conception of the nature of reality, of knowledge, and (eventually) of God that, as one of the eternal philosophical predispositions, seems to lie in opposition to the animating spirit of poetry almost without regard to its subject. This is a philosophical otherworldliness. It tells the poet he is deceived about reality, about the very material he deals with. In its acutest form it says to him, as Augurellius said to Peter Lipomanus (in Henry Vaughan's version):

> Peter, when thou this pleasant world dost see,
> Beleeve, thou seest meere Dreames and vanitie;
> Not reall things, but false: and through the Aire
> Each where, an empty, slipp'rie Scene, though faire.
> The chirping birds, the fresh woods shadie boughes,
> The leaves shrill whispers, when the west-wind blowes.
> The swift, fierce Greyhounds coursing on the plaines,
> The flying hare distrest 'twixt feare and paines;
> The bloomy Mayd decking with flowers her head,
> The gladsome, easie youth by light love lead;
> And whatso'er heere with admiring eyes
> Thou seem'st to see, 'tis but a fraile disguise
> Worne by eternall things, a passive dresse
> Put on by things that are passiveless.[9]

We can feel the real force of this conception if we try turning directly from this to something in, say, *England's Helicon*. How are we now to read those lovely lines:

> Come away, come sweet Love
> The golden morning breakes:
> All the earth, all the ayre,
> Of love and pleasure speakes.[10]

27

If the words stick in our throats, and all our delight turns foolish and embarrassed, we have vitally sensed the nature of the collision that takes place when this otherworldly metaphysic confronts the classical literary tradition; when, in the most poignant instance, the sweet earthly world of the Elizabethan singers meets, in the seventeenth century, the re-awakened otherworldliness of the religious tradition.

What saps the reader's delight in *England's Helicon*, at perhaps the most basic level, is the conception of reality revealed in Augurellius's words. We associate such a conception with the Hellenic contribution to Christianity, and speak of it in terms made familiar by the Platonic philosophical tradition. It is proper to adopt those terms here, and take some notice of the Platonic point of view, for in speaking of Plato and Greek philosophy we are dealing with the ideological foundations of the otherworldly spirit in Christian culture, the philosophical scheme that most obviously provokes and supports the attitude toward the world that makes trouble for poetry. Plato is worth our direct attention for the fact that Christian writers continually cite his argument against poetry to support their own, and for the more important fact that the general Christian attitude toward poetry can be regarded as a kind of emotional equivalent of Plato's theoretical description of poetry's position.

We hold the Platonic tradition responsible for the conception of two orders of existence, a higher and a lower, different in kind, each perceived in different ways. In Plato, we remember, the lower order, the visible world of Change or Becoming, is apprehended by sense-perception. It is temporal, changing, material, and imperfect. The higher order, the realm of Ideas, or Being, is apprehended by the reason. It is eternal, unchanging, immaterial, and perfect. Since the lower order is an image or copy of the higher it is conceived to be less 'real' than its model. Knowledge of the Ideas is the only true knowledge; what we get from the world of Becoming is unreliable opinion. Plato uses this scheme powerfully in his familiar argument against poetry in the *Republic*, showing that the artist, by imitating objects in the world of Becoming, is making only a copy of a copy, and is thus twice-removed from reality—and true knowledge. This metaphysic is understandably not a very popular one with poets, for the conception of an other 'real' world behind this one, apprehensible only by the reason or mystic intuition, seems to destroy the stuff of poetry, the concrete world our senses and feelings respond to. 'Plato', said Yeats, 'thought nature but a spume that plays/Upon a ghostly paradigm of things'.[11] The theory of knowledge accompanying this metaphysic is bound to be discomforting, for it tells us that the senses are untrustworthy guides, misleading the soul in the search for truth. If we begin, as Heraclitus did, with the proposition that the senses deceive while the reason really knows, then our philosophy seems inevitably to arrive at an epistemological distrust of poetry. When this happens we may add a charge to what our religion tells us is bad: it is also false.

But we are not directly concerned here with technical philosophy or argued theories of art. We call up Plato in order to view a representation, in schematic form, of the philosophical otherworldliness that, in various modifications and combinations, gets into Christianity. We are more interested in the otherworldly tendency, in the conception of reality as twofold and opposed, than in any particular formulation of the consequences for art of this conception. For if poetry is necessarily concrete and particular, an invitation to our emotions to react as they react to the world in our original acquaintance with it, i.e., through the senses and feelings rather than through the abstracta evolved by the reason or divined by mystic intuition, if poetry can't help being like this, then any such otherworldly tendency, any 'recognition of an unseen world of unchanging reality behind the flux of phenomena',[12] a spiritual universe superior to the world of appearance, is latently antipathetic to poetry.

We have an indication of the depth of this antipathy by the fact that even poetry written to serve and adore God may be embarrassed by the consequences of philosophical otherworldliness. Trouble here results from the idea of God developed in Christianity by Greek-style philosophizing, the conception of the otherworldly Absolute so different from the pictorially conceived, personal Father of the Hebrew tradition. 'The Semitic peoples were essentially theocratic; they used the forms of the sensuous imagination in setting forth the realities of the unseen world. They were not given to metaphysical speculation. . . . With the Greeks it was far otherwise. . . . Their speculation as to the nature of God had led them gradually to separate Him by an infinite distance from all creation, and to feel keenly the opposition of the finite and the infinite, the perfect and the imperfect, the eternal and the temporal.'[13] The Christian God we inherit is a combination of both Gods. Yet, as Arthur Lovejoy reminds us, 'the God of Aristotle had almost nothing in common with the God of the Sermon on the Mount—though, by one of the strangest and most momentous paradoxes in Western history, the philosophical theology of Christendom identified them, and defined the chief end of man as the imitation of both'.[14]

It is the aspects of God conceived under Hellenic influence that embarrass religious poetry. The trouble is that a Christian poet cannot very well speak directly about the object of worship of his religion if the attributes of that object are 'expressible only in negations of the attributes of this world'.[15] There is nothing for the sensuous imagination to work on, unless, of course, it works indirectly in some allegorical way. Without some such strategy the metaphysically awesome God is always in danger of being reduced and debased by concrete representation. Clearly any view of God that tends to make Him less personal and more mysterious and ineffable, to move Him further and further into the 'other' world, is a potential handicap to religious poetry. What a great handicap it is to Milton to be required to acknowledge in his pictorial poem this Being, the God he by tradition must hail as

> Omnipotent,
> Immutable, Immortal, Infinite,
> Eternal King; thee Author of all being,
> Fountain of Light, thy self invisible . . . [16]

The poet, by the nature of his art, operates in a realm that disqualifies him for the highest vision. Samuel Johnson had something like this in mind when he said, 'The ideas of Christian theology are too simple for eloquence, too sacred for fiction, and too majestic for ornament, to recommend them by tropes and figures is to magnify by a concave mirror the sidereal hemisphere.'[17] To speak like this is not to say that there is no such thing as Christian religious poetry. All this means is that Christian religious poems are properly poems of the experience of religion, not of its object. Even in this proper kind of religious poem, however, the sensuous imagination may be under some suspicion. We sense the difficulty here if we consider the way the believer knows the illimitable God and gives Him his devotion. The relationship is properly simple and direct. 'God is light', and man is illuminated by God's truth primarily through an inner revelation, or mystic intuition, or through written revelation in Scripture. There is nothing devious about either one. Man's devotion should be correspondingly simple and forthright, sincerely showing the condition of his heart; no prayer was ever commended to God by its artfulness. Even for devotional uses, then, the devices of the literary imagination may be suspect, for if a poem must be consciously fashioned, as the literary tradition (i.e. the classical tradition, Horace) would have it, then it hardly serves the spontaneous sincerity of the devout heart, and the love of God needs no artifice or embellishment. We recognize this demand for a 'pure' relationship with God, without mediation, as the core of Puritan belief, and hold it accountable for the characteristic Puritan attitudes toward art, but it is not, of course, limited to Puritans.

We should not, because of our literary sympathies here, end with an unbalanced picture of the kind of piety discussed above. We are concerned with limited aspects of that piety, the aspects that have 'troublesome' consequences for poetry. If these are only the secondary consequences of a kind of vision that, in its primary operation, has given the Western world spiritual insights so dazzlingly compelling as to outweigh all lesser effects, then these observations deserve adjustment in that larger context. The tradition touched on here, the Platonic and Puritan tradition of the illimitable God, is that same strain of piety so impressively described by Perry Miller,[18] the Augustinian strain, the source of

31

Christianity's greatest spiritual insights. We do not mean to disprize the claims of that tradition glancingly.

It may be that the whole Christian impediment to poetry is, for the imagination, best realized in a single image: the fountain of light. When Christ, rejecting the classical world in *Paradise Regained*, says

> he who receives
> Light from above, from the fountain of light,
> No other doctrine needs

we find in His words an apt expression of Hebraic exclusiveness. In the Hebraic sense the 'fountain of light' points to the one true religion; all outsiders dwell in darkness. There is only one fountain, or source, of the matter necessary to a Christian, only one literature in which pleasure is unstained. That comes to us in Christ's 'native language':

> All our Law and Story strew'd
> With Hymns, our Psalms with artful terms inscrib'd,
> Our Hebrew Songs and Harps . . .
> Sion's songs, to all true tasts excelling,
> Where God is prais'd aright, and Godlike men,
> The Holiest of Holies, and his Saints.

The 'fountain of light' is the single and exclusive spring of truth flowing from Sion, the light of guidance given to the chosen people and passed from them. But we may read in the 'fountain of light' another meaning, and think of it in an Hellenic sense too, conveniently uniting in one image both elements antipathetic to poetry. This meaning we find more clearly in the foreground in Milton's other use of the phrase, the passage in *Paradise Lost* where the illimitable God in all his theological attributes is celebrated:

> Thee Father first they sung Omnipotent,
> Immutable, Immortal, Infinite,
> Eternal King; thee Author of all being,
> Fountain of Light, thy self invisible . . .

Here the phrase suggests those neo-Platonic modes of conceiving the deity, the ineffable One who dwells in Light, that have worked into Christian theology and helped give us the metaphysically awesome God we inherit, along with other habits in metaphysic, from Greek philosophy. If we think of the fountain of light in this double sense we may combine the two elements most inimical to poetry, one Hebraic, the other Hellenic, and conceive in one image the fundamental challenge to poetry as sensed most vividly by the Christian imagination.

The practical consequence of this impediment, we know, is that poetry in the classical tradition is condemned on three main counts: (1) it is idle, (2) it is bad, and (3) it is false. These are complaints against the purpose (or source), the matter (or content), and the art (or method) of poetry. The first is a complaint against the unworthy or trivial goal of belles lettres—entertainment—and its uselessness to man in the pursuit of his exclusive and only real goal. Second, poetry is bad because it traffics pleasurably in the world of the senses and feelings; it is infected by the sensuous nature of its material, seductively making 'the too much loved earth more lovely'.[19] Finally, the whole method of such poetry, its art, is false because its inspiration and technique are outside the exclusive Christian channels; it is not a 'sincere' activity of the reason informed by the 'Fountain of Light', and thus purveys trifling fictions rather than God's truth.

As for the term 'classical tradition', what does it mean when we apply it to particular poems? Now, in general, we may have at least three different aspects of a poem in mind when we say that it is in the classical tradition. We may mean merely that it exhibits a great deal of classical allusion, that the author drew on the storehouse of classical mythology to ornament his poem. Or, loosely speaking, we may mean that it is a classical kind of poem, say an epic or pastoral, following classical models either immediately or at a distance. Or we may mean that ideas expressed in the poem are traceable to sources in classical antiquity, to classical philosophy. If we are interested in the relation of classical and Christian elements in the poem, this last meaning must be set apart from the others, for the classical literary tradition and the classical philosophical tradition are different quantities, and each stands in a different relation to Christianity. For one thing, as the preceding discussion reminds us, classical philosophy so permeates what we now know as Christian thought that it is very hard to disentangle the two. Furthermore, if we are concerned with attitudes toward the classical literary tradition, we find that classical philosophy, at least in the Platonic line, is better placed on the Christian side than on the 'classical' side. Plato is against the classical literary tradition in fundamentally the same way that Christian thinkers are. In approaching seventeenth-century poetry from the present perspective, therefore, it should already be clear that the term 'classical' is restricted to the first two meanings; otherwise we confuse the issue with a poet's doctrinal humanism (observed typically, for example, in Milton's debt to Plato) which, though interesting and important, has quite another relation to the Christian elements in his poetry.

In the seventeenth century we recognize an immediate classical tradition that we can understand clearly according to the above meanings. This tradition lies in Elizabethan erotic poetry and its use of classical setting and reference—the tradition of *Hero and Leander* and *Venus and Adonis*, and all the erotic pastorals and epithalamia of the period. There is no doubt, as we enter the seventeenth century, that the classical has taken the print of erotic experience. This, at any rate, is what provoked the most outspoken religious complaints against poetry's paganism. It is the immediate background of the poetry we take up in the seventeenth century, and it further serves to indicate what associations certain kinds of classical allusion might bring into a poem at this time.

Yet, in the seventeenth century, we must become used to a broader conception of the classical tradition than this. Carew, in his famous epitaph for John Donne, exhibits a typical stretching of the notion of the classical:

> Here lies a king, that rul'd as he thought fit
> The universal monarchy of wit;
> Here lie two flamens, and both those the best:
> Apollo's first, at last the true God's priest.[20]

34

Donne was never Apollo's priest in any strict sense. He makes
hardly any classical reference and is praised for expelling the gods
and goddesses from his poetry. Nor does he write in the strict
classical forms. What did Carew mean? He was referring to
Donne's love poetry; as far as a seventeenth-century observer was
concerned, this placed him in the classical literary tradition. We
are justified in shaping our conception of the classical tradition
accordingly. Thus, realizing that there is no absolute classicism,
and no single classical tradition (as Douglas Bush reminds us),[21]
we are not so much concerned with intrinsic qualities in classical
literature, whatever these may be, but with what poets under
particular circumstances make of classical material—not what it
was but what they thought it was. This, I take it, is what we are
properly studying in any tradition.

How the conception of a classical-Christian conflict may be
employed in practical criticism is, in general, not hard to anticipate.
We look for answers to the natural question, 'Given the conflict,
what happens in the poetry?' If there is any aspect of a poem which
a knowledge of the conflict helps us to understand better (or
which helps us to understand the conflict better) then it is worth
using. What we hope for from a perspective like this, of course,
is that good poems will light up, as it were, with new significance.
Then the game is really worth the candle.

In practice, there are two main aspects of the poetry of the
seventeenth century that take on interest through the classical-
Christian conflict. These correspond to the kinds of suspicion that
may be cast on poetry from the Christian perspective. On the one
hand there is the suspicion of the material the poet deals with. If
this material comes from classical mythology it carries the taint
of its suspect pagan origin and of its customary use in the classical
tradition, which in the poetry we shall examine is primarily the
tradition of secular love poetry, the Ovidian tradition. Within the
context of this complaint the original classical material, however
later poets make use of it, retains the capacity to stand for and
suggest the original elements in the conflict, and may take on
through the tension a special affective significance, an extra charge
of association and suggestion. Certain kinds of Christian reference

may also take on new significance against the background of the conflict. This is one of the main reasons the issue is so interesting for the study of particular poems. On the other hand there is the suspicion of the way the poet deals with his material, his artfulness. This sets the Horatian skill and care, the deviousness and embellishment, the imagination and wit—all expended on falsehood—against the sincerity of religious utterance in direct view of divine truth.

In attending to the first aspect, the material of the poetry, I do not mean to say that the relation between classical and Christian elements is always one of conflict. We are not concerned here with the mere *mixture* of classical and Christian material. We are interested only in a particular relation between the two elements, that of conflict, and the intensity and importance of this varies from age to age and poet to poet, never, perhaps, becoming statistically very impressive. In the earlier Renaissance, for example, with the great popularity of classical culture, there is everywhere an easy mixing of the two; only here and there does the older tension show itself. But in the seventeenth century, with the resurgence of the intransigent, otherwordly spirit of the early church, the spirit of the Reformation evidenced partially by Puritanism, with this revival the conflict becomes warm again. After this century the thing is over for good; it subsides completely by the time of the Augustans. But certainly at any time the great mass of classical or mythological reference is merely incidental, a kind of literary swank or slang, innocent of any uniform affective significance. This is of no interest for the present purpose. We shall be concerned only with the occasional outcropping of the conflict that is latent in the mixture of these two traditions.

My own practical applications of this perspective are less grand than may seem promised by the elevated overview I have been enjoying in these pages. My samples of the perspective in use are far from complete, and they may be variously defective as practical criticism. Yet, if the perspective is sound, the deficiencies of the particular critic, and the limitations of his choices, need not condemn the general point of view, which may be employed (and indeed has been employed) fruitfully by other critics. The four poets chosen for examination here are those in which the matter seems to me most interesting. Furthermore, I think a study of their work permits a statement of the issues most significant for the rest of seventeenth-century poetry. The poets are, in a way, representative. The selection cuts across many of the customary groupings of seventeenth-century poetry. There is one, Herbert, from the 'holy' line, following Donne, and one from the 'carnal' line, Herrick. Marvell straddles both lines and Milton, of course, stands in a special position outside either. From the old tripartite division of seventeenth-century poets into the followers of Spenser Jonson, and Donne, there is a representative of each. Donne receives no special treatment for the simple reason that the issue is not immediately significant in his poetry.

Though these essays are held together by the common perspective employed in each, the emphasis naturally varies from poet to poet. In some places the evocative value of classical reference is of chief concern, and one is led to inquire how the suggestions introduced into a poem by such reference operate with respect to Christian attitudes; at the same time, the function of religious terms calls for similar evaluation. The result is particularly worth attention when there is a mixing of vocabularies. The perspective invites an investigation of the use of classical allusion to represent Christian ideas (as, Jove for Jehovah, etc.) or to shut out Christian ideas (as in the love poet's use of a classical atmosphere for a 'moral holiday'). It is proper to ask if there is any strategy to fuse, balance, or reconcile these traditions, and if the tension is a good or bad thing for the poetry. In other places the primary interest lies in the classical or literary manner of a poem, particularly in a poem making a Christian statement. Here the tension is generated by the Christian attitude toward literary artifice, and we look to see how the poet handles this seeming incompatibility of form and matter. The question is of special interest in this period because it is the time of the great effort in English poetry to poetize Biblical subjects. It was, for the most part, an effort that failed, as Sir William Temple, writing at the end of the period (1690), observes:

The Religion of the Gentiles had been woven into the Con-

37

texture of all the antient Poetry with a very agreable mixture, which made the Moderns affect to give that of Christianity a place also in their Poems. But the true Religion was not found to become Fiction so well as a false had done, and all their Attempts of this kind seemed rather to debase Religion than to heighten Poetry.[22]

We are tempted to ask why this should be so, and to assess Milton's handling of the problem.

The issue, of course, has many sides, and no one view exhausts the critical possibilities. It is the kind of issue, clearly, wherein the critic is concerned not so much to argue a thesis as to make an exhibit, to show how a group of poems look from a particular point of view. The enterprise is justified if it helps to a fuller understanding of a worthwhile body of poetry.

Since the following essays are in a measure independent, they will (at the risk of repetitiousness) restate the obvious points made here; the reader need not take them in order nor, necessarily, with close reference to the introduction.

NOTES TO CHAPTER I

[1] *Minor Poets of the Seventeenth Century*, ed. R. G. Howarth (London and New York: Everyman's Library, 1931), p. 140.

[2] Opening lines of CCCLXV, *Sonnets & Songs*, trans. Anna Maria Armi (New York, 1946), pp. 512–3.

[3] H. J. C. Grierson, *Cross Currents in English Literature of the XVIIth Century* (London, 1929), pp. 1–2.

[4] Preface to the translation of *Orlando Furioso* (1591), in *Elizabethan Critical Essays*, ed. G. Gregory Smith (Oxford, 1904), II, 197–8.

[5] Grierson, *Cross Currents*, p. 12.

[6] Holy Sonnets III, in *John Donne: Complete Poetry and Selected Prose*, ed. John Hayward (Bloomsbury, 1929), p. 280.

[7] *Select Letters of St Jerome*, trans. F. A. Wright (London: The Loeb Classical Library, 1954), p. 126.

[8] Bk. IV, lines 221–364. Citations from Milton in my text are to *The Works of John Milton* (New York, 1931–9), the Columbia Milton.

[9] Henry Vaughan, *The Works of Henry Vaughan*, ed. L. C. Martin (Oxford, 1914), I, 214.

[10] *Englands Helicon*, ed. Hugh MacDonald (London, 1950), p. 164.

[11] In *Among School Children*.

[12] William Ralph Inge, *The Platonic Tradition in English Religious Thought* (London, 1926), p. 8.

[13] 'Christianity', *Encyclopaedia Britannica*, 14th edition.

[14] *The Great Chain of Being* (Cambridge, Mass., 1936), p. 5.

[15] *Ibid.*, p. 42.

[16] *Paradise Lost*, III, 372–5.

[17] Cited without source by Joan Bennett, *Four Metaphysical Poets* (Cambridge, England, 1934), p. 125.

[18] Perry Miller, *The New England Mind: The Seventeenth Century* (Cambridge, Mass., 1939), chapter I.

[19] Sidney's phrase in *The Defense of Poesy*.

[20] *Minor Poets of 17th Century*, p. 124.

[21] *Mythology and the Renaissance Tradition in English Poetry* (Minneapolis, 1932), p. 6.

[22] 'Of Poetry', in *Critical Essays of the Seventeenth Century*, ed. J. E. Spingarn (Oxford, 1909), III, 99.

CHAPTER II

Herrick and the Ceremony of Mirth

ఘ

ONE OF THE chief attractions readers have found in Robert Herrick's poetry is the happy, flowering, lover's world that he evokes in poem after poem in *Hesperides*, the collection of his secular poems. It is a world of nature, youth, desire, rural delight, sensuous fragrance, and delicate fable. And it is nearly always a classical world, where all the girls are Antheas and Julias and Corinnas and even the 'sea-scourged merchant' is going to Ithaca. As we respond to these poems we are likely to feel that this association—love, nature, pagan antiquity—is naturally felicitous, even inevitable, and that the classicism is a good thing for the poems and the erotic effects they seek. This invites one to ask just how good a thing it is, and in what way—a simple question with an obvious answer, but worth answering clearly.

Let us consider Herrick's sensuous world at its most exquisite, in *The Apparition of his Mistresse calling him to Elizium*. Here we have nature voluptuous in roses and cassia, ambergris and gums; and nature abundant 'Where ev'ry tree a wealthy issue beares/Of fragrant Apples, blushing Plums or Peares'. It is the unfading garden where 'in green Meddowes sits eternall May'. And it is appropriately the setting where 'naked Younglings, handsome Striplings run':

> And here we'l sit on Primrose-banks, and see
> Love's Chorus led by Cupid; and we'l be
> Two loving followers too unto the Grove,
> Where Poets sing the stories of our love.[1]

Among the company are crowds of poets listening to Homer. Pindar is there and Anacreon whose 'Frantick-Looks, shew him truly Bacchanalian like,/Besmear'd with Grapes.' Ovid lies by Corinna who 'steeps/His eye in dew of kisses while he sleeps'.

If our business is to ask what qualities are given to a poem by such classical reference, the answer here is clear. Herrick is taking advantage of the 'paganism' contained in classical material. The classical atmosphere, or setting, brings with it the 'pagan spirit'. This setting establishes a particular relation to Christian attitudes, indicated in the meaning of 'pagan'—outside the Christian. This is important for Christian writers, and readers, and, indeed, for any milieu in which the audience approaches a work with undeniable allegiance to Christian values—and this is certainly the milieu of seventeenth-century literature. For the classical framework or setting allows a temporary suspension of Christian standards. It may provide, in the modern phrase, a 'moral holiday' in a classical atmosphere. It implies that the action or attitudes are exempt from Christian criteria, particularly that sensuality is free from a Christian sense of sin. It thus helps set the poem in an ethical frame free from normal Christian considerations which, if admitted, might undermine the effect of the poem. This is, of course, a natural and common thing and hardly a conscious programme to baulk moralists. Carew's lovers' Elysium in *A Rapture* is insulated in the same way: 'There shall the Queens of Love and Innocence/Beauty and Nature, banish all offence.'[2] And the *Hesperides* is full of poems in this completely classical frame—*To Electra, Lyrick to Mirth, The Welcome to Sack*—where it works parallel to, and supports, Herrick's flowering natural world.

This is not, however, the only source of reference that works to set off the lover's world in Herrick's poetry. Another interesting component of Herrick's atmosphere of love is the folk-pagan element, the matter of 'the Court of Mab, and of the Fairie-King'. At times this works with the classical reference and at times it works alone to set the atmosphere for the action. The business of the elves in *The Night-piece, to Julia* works this way, I think, casting a permissive fairy light around the tryst where, says the speaker, 'My soule Ile poure into thee':

Her Eyes the Glow-worme lend thee,
The Shooting Starres attend thee;
 And the Elves also,
 Whose little eyes glow,
Like the sparks of fire, befriend thee.

No Will-o'-th'-Wispe mis-light thee;
Nor Snake, or Slow-worme bite thee:
 But on, on thy way
 Not making a stay,
Since Ghost ther's none to affright thee.
. . . .
Then Julia let me wooe thee,
Thus, thus to come unto me:
 And when I shall meet
 Thy silv'ry feet,
My soule Ile poure into thee.

These strategies have such interest for us partly because we know
what challenges they were thwarting, or attempting to thwart. If
this were Ovid, and not a 'let's pretend we're Ovid', there would
be no issue. But we are dealing with a Christian poet who felt the
sense of opposition between his poetry and his religion, as so many
poets of Herrick's century did. The antagonism between the
Christian position and the dominant spirit of the *Hesperides* is most
baldly apparent in the many statements of renunciation in *Noble
Numbers*, the collection of religious poems. A good illustration
from these, 'His pious Pieces', is *His Prayer for Absolution*:

For those my unbaptized Rhimes,
Writ in my wild unhallowed Times;
For every sentence, clause and word,
That's not inlaid with Thee, (my Lord)
Forgive me God, and blot each Line
Out of my Book, that is not Thine.
But if, 'mongst all, thou find'st here one
Worthy thy Benediction;
That One of all the rest, shall be
The Glory of my Work, and Me.

42

Herrick often feels (with one side of him) that God is his proper subject. Yet here he runs into one of the perennial difficulties of the poet who, out of conviction, attempts to write directly about the best subject, God. He is baulked by the very ineffability or philosophical aloofness of the Christian God. He gives his poem the ambitious title *What God is* and then he is stumped and must admit

> God is above the sphere of our esteem,
> And is the best known not defining Him.

Donne described the same problem:

> Eternal God (for whom who ever dare
> Seek new expressions, doe the Circle square,
> And thrust into strait corners of poore wit
> Thee, who art cornerlesse and infinite)
> I would but blesse thy name, not name thee now.[3]

Samuel Johnson expresses the predicament thus: 'Contemplative piety, or the intercourse between God and the human soul, cannot be poetical. Man admitted to implore the mercy of his Creator and plead the merits of his Redeemer is already in a higher state than poetry can confer.'[4]

Even the mention of God in such an inappropriate setting as this book of poetry calls for some excuse. It is a violation of a Christian decorum, and Herrick shows how his lovely, flowering world looks from a pious position in *To God*:

> Pardon me God, (once more I Thee intreat)
> That I have plac'd Thee in so meane a seat,
> Where round about Thou seest but all things vaine,
> Uncircumcis'd, unseason'd, and prophane.
> But as Heavens publike and immortall Eye
> Looks on the filth, but is not soil'd thereby;
> So Thou, my God, may'st on this impure look,
> But take no tincture from my sinfull Book;
> Let but one beame of Glory on it shine,
> And that will make me, and my Work divine.

This is hardly tension; it is outright combat, weighted so heavily to one side that there is no possibility of any contribution from the discredited side. It has its polar opposite the single-minded and undiluted eroticism of many of the poems in *Hesperides*. When both positions are expressed thus it is only possible to alternate between them. Perhaps at the logical, conscious level of thought Herrick as a man could only alternate between these positions. But occasionally, as a poet, he was able to do something else, as we shall see.

First we must notice an effort, even in the *Noble Numbers*, to bring the worlds together, or at least to place his secular muse in some acceptable position. This involves the common conception of poetry as a 'handmaid' to religion. In *His farwell unto Poetrie* there is at first the sense of only irreconcilable alternatives. Poetry is a lover lingeringly relinquished in the moonlight for stern and high reasons:

> I, my desires screw from thee, and directe
> Them and my thoughts to that sublim'd respecte
> And Conscience unto Priest-hood.

'Poetrie', of course, stands for the many aspects of the world Herrick had evoked in his poetry, the natural world of brooks, blossoms, birds, and bowers, of youth, love, nature, and perfumery —the stuff associated with the Ovidian tradition in particular and with the classical literary tradition in general. This is the core of its attraction and the source of its taint. St Jerome, we remember, relinquished his pagan library in the same mood.

The poem is not a pious recantation, however, but a realization of the value of what is lost. The suggestion is made that poetry is a religious passion, though nature, not God, is its object. Herrick says that he and Poetry

> have out-worne
> The fresh and fayrest flourish of the Morne
> With Flame, and Rapture; drincking to the odd
> Number of Nyne, which makes us full with God,

> And In that Misticke frenzie, wee have hurl'de
> (As with a Tempeste) Nature through the worlde
> And In a Whirl-wynd twirld her home, agast
> Att that which in her extasie had past.

Poetry's own immortality is set forth:

> O thou Allmightye Nature, who did'st give
> True heate, whearwith humanitie doth live
> Beyond its stinted Circle; giveing foode
> (White Fame) and Resurrection to the Good . . .
> . . . .
> Homer, Musaeus, Ovid, Maro, more
> Of those god-full prophetts longe before
> Holde their Eternall fiers; and ours of Late
> (Thy Mercie helping) shall resist stronge fate.

And the poem concludes with the familiar idea of poetry as handmaid to religion:

> Knowe yet, (rare soule,) when my diviner Muse
> Shall want a Hand-mayde, (as she ofte will use)
> Bee readye, thou In mee, to wayte uppon her
> Thoughe as a servant, yet a Mayde of Honor.

This gives the appearance of getting the two muses on at least friendly terms. In Herrick's case, however, it seems to me a rather wistful hope to reconcile them on these grounds. The same wistfulness appears, I feel, in something like a conclusion to *Noble Numbers*:

> *To God*
>
> The work is done; now let my Lawrell be
> Given by none, but by Thy selfe, to me:
> That done, with Honour Thou dost me create
> Thy Poet, and Thy Prophet Lawreat.

To call this wistful is not to gainsay the evidence of effort to make the worlds join, to make Apollo's and the true God's priest one. But if it is done, it is not done by writing religious poems *after* the secular poems. The handmaid idea may apply to Milton; it does not apply very well to Herrick. He is not a religious poet.

45

When he brings the method and spirit of his secular muse to the support of a religious subject the result is likely to be travesty:

> *To his Saviour. The New yeers gift.*
> That little prettie bleeding part
>   Of Foreskin send to me:
> And Ile returne a bleeding Heart,
>   For New-yeers gift to thee.
>
> Rich is the Jemme that thou did'st send,
>   Mine's faulty too, and small:
> But yet this Gift Thou wilt commend,
>   Because I send Thee *all*.

The jarring incongruity of subject and tone hardly requires comment. Knowledge of the specific love convention of the exchange of tokens, or of the Petrarchan exchange of hearts, only increases for the reader the grotesque effect. All serious conception of the Circumcision as covenant and symbol (as we have it, for example, in Milton's poem on the Circumcision) is clearly scuttled beyond hope in this approach.

But let us turn now to the sense of a suspect world as it appears in some of the *Hesperides* poems themselves. The first poem, *The Argument of his Book*, is a good place to begin:

> I sing of Brooks, of Blossomes, Birds, and Bowers:
> Of April, May, of June, and July-Flowers.
> I sing of May-poles, Hock-carts, Wassails, Wakes,
> Of Bride-grooms, Brides, and of their Bridall-cakes.
> I write of Youth, of Love, and have Accesse
> By these, to sing of cleanly-Wantonesse.
> I sing of Dewes, of Raines, and piece by piece
> Of Balme, of Oyle, of Spice, and Amber-Greece.
> I sing of Times trans-shifting; and I write
> How Roses first came Red, and Lillies White.
> I write of Groves, of Twilights, and I sing
> The Court of Mab, and of the Fairie-King.
> I write of Hell: I sing (and ever shall)
> Of Heaven, and hope to have it after all.

The poem is not only an 'argument of' his book, in that it states the content; it is also something of an 'argument for' his book in that it defends, or suggests a defence, for the content. We sense this particularly in the defensive, slightly defiant tone of the closing lines. Herrick says, 'I write of Hell'. This begins the seventh statement of subject, each a couplet, each beginning 'I write of' or 'I sing of'. But this is not a new subject; Herrick does not write about Hell. It is a summary of the whole preceding description of his poetry, a kind of wry acceptance of the terms of a pious criticism: such poetry puts one in danger of Hell. The next statement, 'I sing of Heaven', is the same kind of statement and applies to the same poetry, though this is Herrick speaking in his own language, and answering the first statement: Heaven is here too. *Hesperides* cannot easily be divided into hellish poems and heavenly poems. Herrick refers to the same poems, suggesting perhaps that from one point of view they are hellish, from another heavenly, or that heaven and hell are both present. This paradox is seen also in the oxymoron 'cleanly-Wantonnesse', where the adjective works to take the curse from the noun. And last, Herrick hopes for salvation 'after all'. This could mean 'even after all this sin' but it could also mean 'after all is finally assessed', i.e. what goes now as sin may in the final valuation turn out as something else. Here, although we have a recognition of the tainted nature of his material, we do not have a rejection of it, or a sacrifice of its qualities, but an allegiance to it for what it is. Herrick would like to make this world acceptable but these lines suggest that he would do so, not by changing it, but by changing our viewpoint of the hellish and the heavenly.[5]

Another poem that may be read as part of Herrick's effort to make his secular poems acceptable, to remove them from Christian suspicion, is *When he would have his verses read*. First he makes the objection to his poetry appear to be a matter of mood, of the time of day:

> In sober mornings, doe not thou reherse
> The holy incantation of a verse;
> But when that men have both well drunke, and fed,
> Let my Enchantments then be sung, or read.

An objection may be merely temperament, a censorious disposition. The objector is called 'rigid Cato'. (We note how the use of 'Cato' avoids direct conflict with a Christian position.) Herrick suggests that his poetry has its proper function in a perspective that is just as fundamental to man's nature as is his moral perspective. This perspective is induced when 'the Rose raignes', when nature, beauty, and joy appeal to man:

> When Laurell spirts 'ith fire, and when the Hearth
> Smiles to it selfe, and guilds the roofe with mirth;
> When up the Thyrse is rais'd, and when the sound
> Of sacred Orgies flyes, A round, A round.
> When the Rose raignes, and locks with ointments shine,
> Let rigid Cato read these Lines of mine.

Such joy has, Herrick suggests, a religious quality of its own. He will have the songs to Bacchus, the 'sacred orgies', and he will call them sacred, implying a ritual and ceremony in a kind of counter-religion to that of a man who, we might say, in the sober morning has poorly drunk and fed. In this setting his poetry appears as a 'holy incantation', part of the liturgy.

We find these religious terms in other poems, working into Herrick's pagan world. At times the suggested parallel with religion appears to be a fairly superficial play on Christian terms, as in *His Prayer to Ben. Johnson*:

> When I a Verse shall make,
> Know I have praid thee,
> For old Religions sake,
> Saint Ben to aide me.
>
> . . . .
>
> Candles Ile give to thee,
> And a new Altar;
> And thou Saint Ben, shalt be
> Writ in my Psalter.

Yet, although this is playful, it shows how easily Herrick slipped into these terms when treating of his secular world. And, in the

reference to pagan, or pre-Christian religion, there is still a submerged suggestion that this religion represents a 'live option',
a counter religion: 'For old Religions sake.' Insofar as 'old Religion' calls up the qualities of the original pagan life it catches up
the spirit of Ben's tribe and links this spirit with a sympathetic
religion. There is even the suggestion of a kind of re-establishment
of the 'old Religion' among the sons of Saint Ben, the raising of
'a new Altar'. In this same category of surface play on Christian
terms we may place all the 'hymns' to Venus and Cupid, 'vows'
to Mars, 'canticles' to Apollo and Bacchus.

At times there is only an implied analogy to religious values. *To
live merrily, and to trust to Good Verses* is an example of this. Here
the speaker experiences one of those joyful moments 'when the
Rose raignes, and locks with ointments shine'. The parallel to the
situation described in the earlier poem is made specific:

> Now raignes the Rose, and now
> Th' Arabian Dew besmears
> My uncontrolled brow.

It is a time for the mirth associated with earth's flowering.
Appropriately, it is an occasion to toast the classical poets. At the
gayest moment, however, comes the common reminder of death,
a reminder to the worldly celebrant so frequently used for religious
purposes: worldly pleasure is unsubstantial, temporary; therefore
rely not on it but on eternals of the spirit. And Herrick takes the
manner of one finding the serious lesson in mortality; he has found
a 'text'. But the text is not the immortality of the virtuous soul
but the immortality of good poetry. This is the unblessed poet's
equivalent to religious immortality. In other words, death is
conquered not by renouncing the 'frail world' whose beauty dies,
in favour of an everlasting other world, but by realizing most
successfully the beauty and mirth in the natural world. Thus you
do not abjure verses but 'trust to good verses'.

> And when all Bodies meet
> In Lethe to be drown'd;
> Then onely Numbers sweet,
> With endless life are crown'd.

We would be wrong, of course, to take this as an overt and serious challenge to Christian values. It is not a matter of Herrick's questioning the Christian scheme, and we have no right to say that he does. It is more a matter of finding a place, a justification, an acceptance, for other values that Herrick feels intensely but which have no reasoned and recognized sanction.

The last stanza certainly avoids direct conflict with a Christian point of view. The classical scheme of the afterlife, Lethe, etc., is assumed and the whole poem remains in a frame of classical reference. The fact that we have 'Bodies' and not souls meeting at Lethe further insures avoidance of intrusive associations that might point up the departure from the Christian cosmology. But it is not quite a 'moral holiday', even though the classical reference does give it a setting that nourishes the 'pagan spirit'. We see that the poem is not irrelevant to the 'Christian attitude' toward this spirit if we sense the contrast of Herrick's text on mortality with the usual Christian text. It is this that connects it with the half defensive, half defiant tone of *The Argument of his Book*, the mild suggestion that 'idle verse' has its own claims on heaven.

At other times we find religious terms working more subtly on obviously 'pagan' material. One example is the short poem *To Sylvia*:

> I am holy, while I stand
> Circum-crost by thy pure hand:
> But when that is gone; Again,
> I, as others, am Prophane.

This is more than the playful use of religious comparisons for hyperbolic compliment, the practice so common to Elizabethan courtly poets and, as we know, occasional in Herrick too. To appreciate this we might set the poem alongside an Elizabethan conceit employing the religious comparison, an instance excellent and successful in its own right and, at first glance, apparently working the same effect as Herrick's lines. I refer to the Earl of Oxford's 'Heav'n pictur'de in hir face,/Doth promise joy and grace.' Here is the full context:

What cunning can expresse
The favour of hir face,
To whom in this distresse,
I doe appeale for grace,
    A thousand Cupids flie,
    About hir gentle eie.

From whence each throwes a dart,
That kindleth soft sweete fier:
Within my sighing hart,
Possessed by desier:
    No sweeter life I trie,
    Than in hir love to die.

The Lillie in the fielde,
That glories in his white:
For pureness now must yeelde,
And render up his right:
    Heav'n pictur'de in hir face,
    Doth promise joy and grace.[6]

I do not mean to say that the idea of 'heavenly grace' here is without strong effect in its connotations, that it does not give a rich qualification to the conception of the woman. This happens through the religious reference in both poems. But in Oxford's poem the grace, translated to its earthly result, is quite limited and works no change in the speaker or his world. And his world, we might add, with its 'soft, sweet fier . . . possessed by desier', is quite vulnerable to a religious criticism. Herrick's religious conception, however, does work a fundamental change. He is sanctified by his lover whose arm around him makes a cross, or sign of a cross, and blesses their relationship. The word 'pure' here then has an added meaning. As an epithet for mistresses it is standard for beauty, whiteness. But in this context it also conveys the idea of religious purity, unstained innocence. The poem as a whole recalls the world of Donne's lovers; Herrick often reminds us more of Donne than of Jonson—a point to remember when we use such labels as 'tribe of Ben'.

The religious suggestions are fundamental in *To the Water Nymphs drinking at the Fountain*:

> Reach, with your whiter hands, to me,
>   Some Christall of the Spring;
> And I, about the Cup shall see
>   Fresh Lillies flourishing.

> Or else sweet Nimphs do you but this;
>   To' th' Glasse your lips encline;
> And I shall see by that one kisse,
>   The Water turn'd to Wine.

The familiar English scene of village maids drawing water has apparently inspired this poem. Herrick is attracted to the beauty of the girls in this setting, and, calling the country girls 'nymphs', he casts them and the scene into the perspective of his classical world. Their charm and beauty are felt by the speaker (and the reader) to convey the appeal of that world; in fact, they minister that enchantment to him when they give him the cup. Notice the quality of this enchantment:

> And I, about the Cup shall see
>   Fresh Lillies flourishing.

We cannot miss the overtones of the Eucharist in the presentation of the cup nor the general suggestion of Christian service in the 'Fresh Lillies flourishing', which calls up many religious associations. Yet it is the whiter hands, the bodily beauty and grace, that are the lilies; they, with all their sensual significance, are the power that perform the miracle. The last stanza repeats even more forcefully the pattern of the first. Here the 'Water turn'd to Wine' makes the girls priestesses in a miraculous transformation recalling Christ's miracle; the enchanted world of the nymphs is evoked by a religious miracle. But here, too, the sensual quality is not diminished but intensified by the very religious terms that at the same time transform and remove the experience from the crudely or purely sensual. The erotic attraction is simultaneous and strong.

The water is turned to wine partly because the lips are 'ruby' lips, as the lilies were brought forth by the 'whiter hands'; the miraculous act is a kiss.

This is no mere alternative to the religious position, at least not in the way the alternative is usually seen. Here, the use of terms drawn from the religious vocabulary works to remove Herrick's natural world from purely sensual indulgence. It may, in the end, tend to modify the destructive antithesis with the Christian position. But the source of the appeal of that world, its sensual attraction, is not sacrificed but intensified at the same time that it is elevated. From this elevation it is a stronger competitive force against the religious challenge, for it is conceived religiously too; as a ceremonial order of experience it is less vulnerable to the attack that sees it as a wanton departure from order. One more poem may illustrate this:

To the Lark

Good speed, for I this day
Betimes my Mattens say:
   Because I doe
   Begin to wooe:
   Sweet singing Lark,
   Be thou the Clark,
   And know thy when
   To say, Amen.
   And if I prove
   Blest in my love;
   Then thou shalt be
   High-Priest to me,
   At my returne,
   To Incense burne;
And so to solemnize
Love's, and my Sacrifice.

In these last three poems we are asking the same kind of question we began with, questioning then the affective value of classical reference. Now, from the opposite direction, we ask, what do these *religious* terms introduce into the poem? They obviously suggest a kind of blessedness in the lover's world—an idea that reminds us of a similar conception in Donne's 'love's-saints' poems. They show us that this order of experience may also be conceived in religious terms; it has aspects that parallel the religious order. Herrick argues the claims of the sensual experience by using religious terms; he puts the experience in competition with religion by using the religious terms themselves. The two orders of experience may be seen in contrast but it is not the kind of contrast that we have between the wantonly carnal and the spiritual, the contrast the Christian easily makes. It may be less a contrast than a general subsuming or admittance of Herrick's flowering world into that religious conception of experience that is the basis of his undeniable belief as a person. The religious terms work partly to cast an acceptable colour over the experience, but primarily they heighten and transform it, giving it a ritual and ceremonial formulation, without sacrificing its essential quality.[7]

Herrick does this with some of the seemingly most mundane aspects of the worldly experience he presents with such gusto. Consider the little poem, *Meat without mirth*:

> Eaten I have; and though I had good cheere,
> I did not sup, because no friends were there.
> Where Mirth and Friends are absent when we Dine
> Or Sup, there wants the Incense and the Wine.

Here the mirth that is of such recurring importance to Herrick is heightened by the ceremonial conception. 'Incense and the Wine' suggests the religious service. The phrase daringly implies in this communion of friends a kind of 'holy communion'. In other words, human conviviality, the mirthful, is comparable to the holy. Herrick's mirthful world, experienced with its own ceremony, does not allow a simple polarity of the natural and the spiritual—a polarity that is inevitably, by customary Christian belief, detrimental to the natural. For in these poems man is not just of nature; to approach the natural world in the ceremonial way is, in fact, not 'natural' in the sense that 'natural' links man to the animal creation. It manifests something distinctive in his *human* nature, something that is comparable to a parallel manifestation of his human nature in its religious expression.

Once we realize the fundamental part these religious terms play in Herrick's conception of his secular world we are conscious of religious overtones in other poems, which, taken in isolation, might not alert us to the issue, but, viewed in the context of Herrick's whole work, suddenly take on a new significance. *His returne to London* is one of these:

> From the dull confines of the drooping West,
> To see the day spring from the pregnant East,
> Ravisht in spirit, I come, nay more, I flie
> To thee, blest place of my Nativitie!
> Thus, thus with hallowed foot I touch the ground,
> With thousand blessings by thy Fortune crown'd.
> O fruit-full Genius! that bestowest here
> An everlasting plenty, yeere by yeere.
> O Place! O People! Manners! fram'd to please
> All Nations, Customes, Kindreds, Languages!
> I am a free-born Roman; suffer then,
> That I amongst you live a Citizen.
> London my home is: though by a hard fate sent
> Into a long and irksome banishment;
> Yet since cal'd back; henceforward let me be,
> O native countrey, repossest by thee!
> For, rather than I'le to the West return,
> I'le beg of thee first here to have mine Urn.
> Weak I am grown, and must in short time fall;
> Give thou my sacred Reliques Buriall.

The occasion of the poem is Herrick's return to London in 1647 following his ejection by the Puritans from his parish in Devonshire. It was, in effect, a return from the priesthood to a secular life; Herrick apparently assumed layman's dress and desired to appear before the public as a layman—as the addition of 'esq.' after his name on the title-page of his book of poems the following year suggests.[8] In the poem the return is conceived as a pilgrimage to a holy city, a 'blest place' touched by a 'hallowed foot'. The 'pregnant East' is not only the place of sunrise from which the day springs but it also suggests the ancient source of religions. This is rather startling when we remember Herrick's situation: he is coming *from* the service of God to secular life in the city. The city thus enshrines the secular delights that Herrick returns to as a religious devotee. London furthermore has a local deity in a fully pagan conception: 'O fruit-full Genius! that bestowest here/An everlasting plenty, yeere by yeere.' The symbolic return to a lost religion is further associated with classical paganism in the identification of London with Rome and Herrick's claim to be a Roman. This religious conception of secular values provides a unifying perspective on all the elements in the natural world that Herrick was attracted to; it shows how deeply he valued them, not only in that they each brought pleasure but in that they represented a coherent order of experience, an order that in his poetry could be grasped whole by the imagination, however fragmented and disordered it might appear to the moral judgment in plain Christian daylight.

The competition of this pagan counter religion with Christianity is not much below the surface here. Viewing Herrick's worshipful return to the secular city and knowing the facts of his situation, we see what a reversal is achieved in his use of religious terms. The 'long and irksome banishment' in the 'dull confines of the drooping West' actually represents his service to God in the priesthood, his normally and officially holy life. Seldom in Herrick is the conflict this open.

Not only does Herrick introduce Christian or religious suggestions into his pagan world, he also moves in the other direction and involves Christian subjects in the atmosphere of his mirthful natural world. In *Ceremonies for Christmasse* the Christmas 'ceremony' means the same old ceremony of mirth in the same spirit:

> Come, bring with a noise,
> My merrie merrie boyes,
> The Christmas Log to the firing;
> While my good Dame, she
> Bids ye all be free;
> And drink to your hearts desiring.

With the last yeeres brand
Light the new block, And
For good successe in his spending,
On your Psaltries play,
That sweet luck may
Come while the Log is a teending.

Drink now the strong Beere,
Cut the white loafe here,
The while the meat is a shredding;
For the rare Mince-Pie
And the Plums stand by
To fill the Paste that's a kneading.

Here the 'pagan spirit' is accommodated to and joins, without
tension, the joy of the Christmas season. In a sense the 'raigne of
the Rose' and the Christian reign are united.

Likewise, in *Ceremonies for Candlemasse Eve*, the ceremony is
almost a rite of nature. Within the Christian celebration we recognize Herrick's 'flowering world':

Down with the Rosemary and Bayes,
Down with the Misleto;
In stead of Holly, now up-raise
The greener Box (for show).

The Holly hitherto did sway;
Let Box now domineere;
Untill the dancing Easter-day,
Or Easters Eve appeare.

Then youthfull Box which now hath grace,
Your houses to renew;
Grown old, surrender must his place,
Unto the crisped Yew.

When Yew is out, then Birch comes in,
And many Flowers beside;
Both of a fresh and fragrant kinne,
To honour Whitsontide.

> Green Rushes then, and sweetest Bents
>   With cooler Oken Boughs;
> Come in for comely ornaments,
>   To re-adorn the house.
> Thus times do shift; each thing his turne
>   do's hold;
> New things succeed, as former things grow old.

The ceremony of mirth receives its fullest expression, however, in one poem, *Corinna's going a-maying*. It is not necessary to dwell in great detail on its mingling of Christian and pagan elements; the poem has, for this, caught the attention of many critics and has been expertly analysed by Cleanth Brooks.[9] Brooks points out, in the flowers bowing to the East, in the birds saying matins and singing hymns, in the village houses becoming 'arks' and 'tabernacles', that the May Day rites are conceived 'as religious rites, though, of course, those of a pagan religion'. It is a 'sin' and 'profanation' to abstain from these rites of nature. Use of the word 'sin' in this way, a near reversal of common Christian application, points up a 'clash between the Christian and pagan world views'. Man's relation to nature is significant in this. 'Corinna', says Brooks, 'is actually being reproached for being late to church—the church of nature. The village itself has become a grove, subject to the laws of nature. One remembers that the original sense of "pagan" was "country-dweller" because the worship of the old gods and goddesses persisted longest there. On this May morning, the country has come into the village to claim it, at least on this one day, for its own. Symbolically, the town has disappeared and its mores are superseded.' These elements qualify the theme in that 'the poem is obviously not a brief for the acceptance of the pagan ethic so much as it is a statement that the claims of the pagan ethic—however much they may be overlaid—exist, and on occasion emerge, as on this day'. Corinna, who is told to 'Rise; and put on your Foliage' along with the other 'budding' boys and girls 'is subject to nature, and to the claims of nature. . . . Not to respond is to "sin" against nature itself.' Brooks points out, finally, a 'reconcilement of the conflicting claims of paganism and Christianity' in 'the village boys and girls with their grass-stained gowns, coming to the priest to receive the blessing of the church':

And some have wept, and woo'd, and plighted Troth,
And chose their priest, ere we can cast off sloth.

All this amounts to a most mature and compelling expression of the *carpe diem* theme.

It is, withal, necessary to emphasize one point about the use of religious terms in this poem, for their effect may be misunderstood. We have seen in some preceding poems that the claims of Herrick's natural world are often made compelling as a kind of parallel or counter religion. In this kind of poem the claims are, in a sense, made *against* a Christian conception of experience. In *Corinna*, however, which is the best of the ceremony poems, the tendency is very much toward *inclusion* in a Christian conception—without a sacrifice of any of the vital qualities of the pagan world. Certainly the pagan attitude gets its due. At first glance the poem may seem like a love poet's parody of a religious poem, sensual love receiving an ironic sort of sanction by a witty reversal of sin and virtue wherein the terms of worship are applied to this pagan activity. But the poem is not a parody. The 'sin' is not religious piety; if we take the literal interpretation, sloth, if anything, is the sin. The matins that the birds say and the hymns they sing are not just rites of nature; we have no reason to believe they are not sincerely Christian too. 'Few beads are best', but the beads are still said. They are not the alternative to this activity. Finally, the wooing ends with the choice of a priest for marriage.

Such mirth is thus not licence, as the typical *carpe diem* poem would have it, nor is it to be abjured, as strict Christian moralism might have it. At the same time that the poem works against the narrowly pious attitude in Christianity, it makes some use of the undeniable wisdom in the Christian order of life, including its action within some lawful boundary and recognizing considerations that are entirely foreign to the classical *carpe diem* statement. So we have 'harmless folly', 'cleanly wantonness', and fun that ends in marriage. The classical *carpe diem* argument which abounds in Elizabethan and Cavalier lyrics makes an illuminating contrast when set alongside Herrick's treatment of the theme. Consider first Ben Jonson's *Song to Celia*:

> Come my Celia, let us prove,
> While we may, the sports of love;
> Time will not be ours, for ever:
> He, at length, our good will sever.
> Spend not then his guifts in vaine.
> Sunnes, that set, may rise againe:
> But if once we loose this light,
> 'Tis, with us, perpetual night.
> Why should we deferre our joyes?
> Fame, and rumor are but toyes.
> Cannot we delude the eyes
> Of a few poore houshold spyes?
> Or his easier eares beguile,
> So removed by our wile?
> 'Tis no sinne, loves fruit to steale,
> But the sweet theft to reveale:
> To be taken, to be seene,
> These have crimes accounted beene.[10]

The customary end of the argument is adulterous seduction, a goal unchanged from Catullus to Jonson. With this we may compare Herrick's famous *To the Virgins, to make much of Time*. The first three stanzas proceed in the normal way:

> Gather ye Rose-buds while ye may,
>   Old Time is still a flying:
> And this same flower that smiles to day,
>   To morrow will be dying.
>
> The glorious Lamp of Heaven, the Sun,
>   The higher he's a getting;
> The sooner will his Race be run,
>   And neerer he's to Setting.
>
> That Age is best, which is the first,
>   When Youth and Blood are warmer;
> But being spent, the worse, and worst
>   Times still succeed the former.

But the fourth stanza puts in place of the usual enticement a word quite foreign to the classical *carpe diem* poem: 'marry'.

> Then be not coy, but use your time;
> And while ye may, goe marry:
> For having lost but once your prime,
> You may for ever tarry.

The end in marriage, the sound advice against becoming an old maid, corresponds to the choosing of a priest after the frolic in *Corinna*. Herrick is able to make the *carpe diem* argument, and do some justice to it, yet end within the Christian fold.

In conclusion it must be remembered that this effort either to compete on even terms or to reconcile the 'pagan spirit' with religious attitudes is not anything like a consistent programme in Herrick's poetry. The proportion of poems in which it appears is small. A great many of the poems in *Hesperides* may be mere erotic 'indulgence' as they have been called. But we need not require a conscious and consistent formulation on the part of the poet. What gives these occasional poems their special interest and, I think, excellence, is that in them we do not have purely erotic or voluptuous effects but we have the various manifestations of the 'pagan spirit'—nature, love, fairy lore, verse, wine, mirth— conceived as an order of experience, an order deserving ritual, ceremony, and art. It is this ceremonial quality, a ritual elevation, that helps give this experience a value beyond that of immediate pleasure. The worth of this kind of experience is most frequently realized or defined against the opposition or resistance, often implicit, of common Christian attitudes. The opposition stands against both the 'pagan ethic' and the classical literary tradition. This is what we mean when we speak of a tension between Christian and classical traditions. It is not present in the mass of purely erotic poems, such as *The Vine* or the various anatomies of woman. Nor is it really present in the many recantations Herrick makes in the *Noble Numbers*, at least not as a fruitful source of definition and understanding of complex and paradoxical values. It is most fruitful in those poems which are neither complete renunciations nor simple paeans of joy, but in which some effort is made to assert the claims of one order of experience without denying the certain and recognized value of another order. This, I take it, is what occurs in *Corinna*.

NOTES TO CHAPTER II

[1] Citations from Herrick in my text are to *The Poetical Works of Robert Herrick*, ed. F. W. Moorman (Oxford, 1915).

[2] *Minor Poets of the 17th Century*, ed. R. G. Howarth (London and New York: Everyman's Library, 1931), p. 103.

[3] *John Donne: Complete Poetry and Selected Prose*, ed. John Hayward (Bloomsbury, 1929), p. 302.

[4] Cited without source by Joan Bennett, *Four Metaphysical Poets* (Cambridge, England, 1934), p. 118.

[5] It may be objected here that *The Argument of his Book* applies not just to the *Hesperides* but to both *Hesperides* and *Noble Numbers*, since they were published originally in the same book, thus making 'I sing of Heaven' more simply explained as a reference to the *Noble Numbers*. It is true that the *Argument* is the first poem in the volume but the fact that in the original edition of 1648 the sacred poems have a separate title page, and even a separate date (1647), would indicate that Herrick considered the poem as an introduction to the *Hesperides*, the first book only, where it appears after the separate title to that book. See F. W. Moorman, *Robert Herrick* (London, 1910), p. 107. This evidence is necessary only if we are unwilling to believe that the whole burden of the poem obviously applies only to the love poems, which I think it does.

[6] *The Phoenix Nest*, 1593, ed. Hyder E. Rollins (Cambridge, Mass., 1931), p. 62.

[7] Thomas R. Whitaker, 'Herrick and the Fruits of the Garden', *ELH*, XXII (March, 1955), 16–33, using a different set of Herrick's poems, has, among other fine insights, exhibited the ceremony in Herrick's paganism. His work is, I believe, the first to do justice to Herrick's poetry from this perspective.

[8] See Moorman, *op. cit.* (above, note 5), p.110.

[9] *The Well Wrought Urn* (New York, 1947), pp. 62–73.

[10] *Poems of Ben Jonson*, ed. George B. Johnston (London, 1954), p. 84.

CHAPTER III

George Herbert's Language of Devotion

THE POETRY of George Herbert would seem to have little to do with the classical tradition as we know it in, say, Jonson and Herrick. Herbert makes practically no reference to classical mythology and, indeed, is widely praised, with Donne, for evicting the gods and goddesses from English poetry. His followers saw him as the leader in the effort to turn poetry to sacred uses. In spirit, of course, his poetry provides the sharpest possible contrast to that of Herrick in the *Hesperides*; yet we may recognize in Herbert a kind of negative relation to poetry in the classical literary tradition. There is no better illustration of this than the first of his *Sonnets* to his mother:

> My God, where is that ancient heat toward thee,
>   Wherewith whole showls of Martyrs once did burn,
>   Besides their other flames? Doth Poetry
> Wear Venus Livery? only serve her turn?
> Why are not Sonnets made of thee? and layes
>   Upon thine Altar burnt? Cannot thy love
>   Heighten a spirit to sound out thy praise
> As well as any she? Cannot thy Dove
> Out-strip their Cupid easily in flight?
>   Or, since thy wayes are deep, and still the same,
>   Will not a verse run smooth that bears thy name?
> Why doth that fire, which by thy power and might
>   Each breast does feel, no braver fuel choose
>   Than that, which one day Worms may chance refuse?[1]

We notice how this complaint, heard so often in the seventeenth century, includes in its objection to love poetry an underlying objection to the classical source of inspiration with which the love poetry is associated. The Christian Dove versus Cupid here as the angel's wing versus the sparrow's plume in Barnabe Barnes's poem:

> No more lewde laies of lighter loves I sing,
>> Nor teach my lustfull Muse abus'de to flie
> With sparrowes plumes, and for compassion crie
> To mortall beauties, which no succour bring.
> But my Muse, fethered with an angel's wing,
>> Divinely mounts aloft unto the skie,
>> Where her Love's subjects with my hopes doe lie.[2]

The rejected muse flies with the wings of Venus' bird, the sparrow, in contrast to the muse of divine inspiration, 'fethered with an angel's wing'. Of further interest in Herbert's poem is the concern over the appropriateness of 'deep' religious truth expressed in poetry: 'Or, since thy wayes are deep, and still the same,/ Will not a verse run smooth that bears thy name?' This is an important issue for Herbert, and we shall turn to it in detail later.

For the moment we can notice how much is contained in these contrasts of the two subjects poetry may treat, and how much the rejected member of the contrast appears in a classical reference that seems to catch up the whole spirit and attitude opposed to the Christian conception. The devotional poet, in fact, is taking advantage of the same affective value latent in classical material that Herrick uses to such an opposite purpose in the *Hesperides*. Consider how the cypress-bays, roses-yew combinations work in a poem by Henry Vaughan, *Idle Verse*, condensing the whole fundamental conflict into one image:

> Go, go, queint folies, sugred sin . . .

> Blind, desp'rate fits, that study how
>> To dresse and trim our shame,
> That gild rank poyson, and allow
>> Vice in a fairer name . . .

> Let it suffice my warmer days
>   Simper'd and shin'd on you;
> Twist not my Cypresse with your Bays,
>   Or Roses with my Yewgh.[3]

In *Mount of Olives* Vaughan uses a contrast that touches particularly the differences of inspiration, setting Christ's Mount against the Hill of the Muses:

> Sweete, sacred hill! on whose fair brow
>   My Savior sate, shall I allow
>   Language to love
> And idolize some shade or grove,
> Neglecting thee? . . .
>
> But thou sleep'st in a deepe neglect,
> Untouch't by any; and what need
> The sheep bleat thee a silly lay,
>   That heard'st both reed
>   And sheepward play?
> Yet if poets mind thee well,
> They shall find thou art their hill,
>   And fountaine too . . . [4]

One of the most powerfully evocative of these pairs is the contrast of crowns, on one side the laureate crown or crown of bays and on the other the crown of thorns. In Donne's *La Corona* the speaker makes a 'crown of prayer and praise' for God, then asks

> But doe not, with a vile crowne of fraile bayes,
> Reward my muses white sincerity,
> But what thy thorny crowne gain'd, that give mee,
> A crowne of Glory, which doth flower alwayes.[5]

The bays are given for an earthly and mortal achievement; this may be an artistic accomplishment but it is not to be credited or compared with the sincerity of the soul in 'prayer and praise'. We notice how often the idea of religious sincerity, even in 'harsh numbers', lies behind the derogation of classical literary art. The preferred crown is the immortal 'crowne of Glory' which, in contrast to the temporal recognition that fades like the world of the senses the poet treats, 'doth flower alwayes'. The poet's crown is part of the 'brittle world'.

Carew, in one of the periodic repentant moments of the love poets, uses the same contrast in the poem noted earlier, *To . . . George Sandys . . . On His Translation of the Psalms:*

> Then I no more shall court the verdant bay,
> But the dry leafless trunk on Golgotha,
> And rather strive to gain from thence one thorn,
> Than all the flourishing wreaths by laureates worn.[6]

This declaration, even in the contrast it insists upon, reveals a kind of submerged recognition of qualities on the side of the 'bay' that appeal to the poet. It is 'verdant', suggesting that for the poet its world is fertile, productive, natural, while the alternative, though the true object of man's striving, is dry and leafless. We can, surprisingly enough, observe this subtle recognition of mixed values in Henry Vaughan. His poem quoted above, *Idle Verse,* concludes as follows:

> Twist not my Cypresse with your Bays,
> Or Roses with my Yewgh.
>
> Go, go, seek out some greener thing;
> It snows and freezeth here;
> Let Nightingales attend the spring;
> Winter is all my year.

This recognizes the association of nature and classicism in secular poetry and realizes the quality of its attraction in 'nightingales' and 'greener things', rejecting it, of course, for the sterner world of moral decision. We can imagine how the 'classical' Herrick, accepting the terms of the contrast as here given, would happily follow the ironic advice of the last stanza.

There is even, I think, a suggestion of the bays-thorn contrast of crowns in Herbert's *The Collar.* The crown of bays appears with its usual connotations:

> Is the yeare onely lost to me?
> Have I no bayes to crown it?
> No flowers, no garlands gay? all blasted?
> All wasted?

The suggestion of the crown of thorns is a secondary association in lines the primary meaning of which concerns mortification of the flesh:

> Have I no harvest but a thorn
> To let me bloud, and not restore
> What I have lost with cordiall fruit?

The attractive sensual alternative to the denial of the flesh appears several times in the image of nature's verdant attractions—flowers, garlands, corn, fruit. The 'pagan' quality evoked by the classical crown of bays works naturally parallel to this—as we remember it in Herrick. Yet, even before the final declaration of faith, we sense that this alternative is impossible for the speaker. The very conception of the attraction as 'fruit' betrays the place of 'natural' pleasure in the speaker's mind even at the moment of greatest rebellion:

> . . . but there is fruit,
> And thou hast hands.

It is the fruit of temptation, the fruit of the garden. We are thus further prepared for the obedient answer to God's voice in the final lines.

One element in these recurring contrasts, we have noticed, is an underlying objection to the classical source of inspiration with which the love poetry is associated. This objection is more than a suspicion of the pagan origin; it includes a distrust of the artifice of poetry, of wit and invention exercised on pleasing fictions. We have observed how this artfulness is inimical to the admiration for religious sincerity, the simple truths that need no decoration. Ornament is not only unnecessary, it is evidence of the unworthy appeal of sensuous attractions. Christ's truth is bare and simple:

But when I view abroad both Regiments;
>> The worlds, and thine:
Thine clad with simplenesse, and sad events;
>> The other fine,
Full of glorie and gay weeds,
>> Brave language, braver deeds;
That which was dust before, doth quickly rise,
>> And prick mine eyes.
>>>> (Herbert, *Frailtie*)

The relation of his art to his belief thus may become a critical issue for a religious poet, particularly when there is a great impetus to turn poetry to religious subjects. Wit should not be necessary. This develops into a point of some strain in Herbert, as we shall see.

Let us begin with the well-known Jordan poems, Herbert's outstanding expression of the desire for simple spiritual sincerity in preference to the deviousness of poetic art.

Jordan (I)

Who sayes that fictions onely and false hair
Become a verse? Is there in truth no beautie?
Is all good structure in a winding stair?
May no lines passe, except they do their dutie
>> Not to a true, but painted chair?

Is it no verse, except enchanted groves
And sudden arbours shadow course-spunne lines?
Must purling streams refresh a lovers loves?
Must all be vail'd, while he that reades, divines,
>> Catching the sense at two removes?

Shepherds are honest people; let them sing:
Riddle who list, for me, and pull for Prime:
I envie no mans nightingale or spring;
Nor let them punish me with losse of rime,
>> Who plainly say, *My God, My King.*

The title 'Jordan' is significant for the theme of the poem, though its exact meaning has been much debated. Apparently its primary significance here is 'baptismal cleansing', a consecration of poetry to purposes that suggest an ascent of the Hebraic over the classical. Jordan makes a neat antithesis to Helicon. But this is in the background; the primary significance is in the sacramental cleansing. Cowley uses the term for the same effect in comment on his *Davideis*: 'Amongst all holy and consecrated things which the Devil ever stole and alienated from the service of the Deity . . . there is none that he so universally, and so long usurpt, as Poetry . . . It is time to Baptize it in Jordan, for it will never become clean by bathing it in the Water of Damascus.'[7] There is also a parallel in Thomes Lodge's preface to *Prosopopeia*: 'Now at last after I have wounded the world with too much surfet of vanitie, I maye bee by the true Helizeus, cleansed from the leprosie of my lewd lines, and beeing washed in the Jordan of grace, imploy my labour to the comfort of the faithfull.'[8]

What damaging arguments against poetry are implicit in Herbert's first stanza: poetry deals with trifling fictions, lies; its beauty is separate from truth; it turns the plain sense to indirection, concealing meaning. These are, in fact, the complaints we associate with Platonic criticism and we are not surprised to find them representative of Christian criticism too. The last two lines recall specifically the Platonic doctrine of imitation which so discredits poetry: 'May no lines passe, except they do their dutie/Not to a true, but painted chair.' Poetry, working through the senses, imitates at a third remove from reality. The senses deceive, but reason, or religious insight, knows truth.

In *Jordan* (II), at one time titled *Invention*, the artistry of the poet appears as a needless bustle:

> When first my lines of heav'nly joyes made mention,
> Such was their lustre, they did so excell,
> That I sought out quaint words and trim invention;
> My thoughts began to burnish, sprout, and swell,
> Curling with metaphors a plain intention,
> Decking the sense, as if it were to sell.
>
> Thousands of notions in my brain did runne,
> Off'ring their service, if I were not sped:

I often blotted what I had begunne;
This was not quick enough, and that was dead.
Nothing could seem too rich to clothe the sunne,
Much lesse those joyes which trample on his head.

As flames do work and winde, when they ascend,
So did I weave myself into the sense.
But while I bustled, I might heare a friend
Whisper, How wide is all this long pretence!
There is in love a sweetnesse readie penn'd:
Copie out onely that, and save expense.

All of the devices that make for excellence in the literary tradition seem misapplied when the subject is heavenly joy. The religious intention is properly 'plain' and direct, needing no ornament or indirection of metaphor. Here is the Platonic, and Christian, emphasis on content, the truth that passes through (possesses, we might say) the writer, whose style and artistry are irrelevant. Coming to the surface in Herbert's poetry is the same sort of conflict we have between Horace and Plato, between the classical literary tradition and the Platonic philosophical tradition, between art and Puritanism. If the sweetness consists in what is 'readie penn'd' then the poet's skill and care as a 'maker' of the poem is just a 'long pretence'.

In *The Forerunners* the loss of the 'sparkling notions' of poetry is forecast by whitening hair, which appears in the figure of death's harbinger chalking the door. Yet, despite intellectual decay, the simple statement, 'Thou art still my God', is still possible to the poet and, indeed, the best of all language: 'He will be pleased with that dittie;/And if I please him, I write fine and wittie.' The language of poetry is not scorned but is rather regretfully relinquished:

Farewell sweet phrases, lovely metaphors.
But will ye leave me thus? when ye before
Of stews and brothels onely knew the doores,
Then did I wash you with my tears, and more,
    Brought you to Church well drest and clad:
My God must have my best, ev'n all I had.

The 'stews and brothels' from which poetic language was rescued and converted is not any personal confession of Herbert's past; it figures the lascivious end of love poetry. In this personification the art of poetry has become something separate from the material of poetry, and thus it becomes a kind of guiltless thing whose beauties may be attracted and used by either side, the Church's and the world's. The personification continues in the fourth and fifth stanzas:

> Lovely enchanting language, sugar-cane,
> Hony of roses, whither wilt thou flie?
> Hath some fond lover tic'd thee to thy bane?
> And wilt thou leave the Church, and love a stie?
>   Fie, thou wilt soil thy broider'd coat,
> And hurt thy self, and him that sings the note.

> Let foolish lovers, if they will love dung,
> With canvas, not with arras, clothe their shame:
> Let follie speak in her own native tongue.
> True beautie dwells on high: ours is a flame
>   But borrowed thence to light us thither.
> Beautie and beauteous words should go together.

This is not quite the same attitude that we have in the Jordan poems. There we found that the 'art' in poetry is regretted, that metaphors should not curl a plain intention, that the simple 'My God, My King' is best. Here the simple devotional statement indicating faith is still the most important requirement. But an aid, not a hindrance, is lost when poetry's language leaves. God also represents 'true beautie' and 'Beautie and beauteous words should go together.' The poem ends, however, with a restatement of the theme of simple faith; what poetry can add is only peripheral embellishment:

> Yet if you go, I passe not; take your way:
> For, *Thou art still my God*, is all that ye
> Perhaps with more embellishment can say.
> Go birds of spring; let winter have his fee;
>   Let a bleak paleness chalk the doore,
> So all within be livelier then before.

Herbert at different times makes really two requests. At one time he seems to be asking, 'Why can't we turn all the fine language of poetry from its common idle uses to the support and expression of religious truth?' At another time he says, 'The fine language of poetry is a distracting irrelevance in religious expression; the simple statement of devotion is the highest poetry.' There is some difficulty in meeting these requirements. Apparently, for reasons we have noted, a good Christian could not be comfortable following the first course. And we can legitimately question whether a good poet, or any poet, could follow the second.

The fact is that Herbert's allegiance to the second point of view was more official than real. For all that he has been praised for his manliness and simplicity, in practice Herbert did not follow this advice. He seldom says simply, 'My God, My King', and his plain intention is always curled with metaphors, even in the very poems that reject this strategy. Several of Herbert's most admired devotional poems, even on doctrinal subjects, are as thickly clotted with metaphor as any by the other metaphysical poets. Witness, for example, the poem *Sunday*, which in this connection it is difficult to resist quoting at length:

> O Day most calm, most bright,
> The fruit of this, the next worlds bud,
> Th' indorsement of supreme delight,
> Writ by a friend, and with his bloud;
> The couch of time; cares balm and bay;
> The week were dark, but for thy light:
> Thy torch doth show the way.

> The other dayes and thou
> Make up one man; whose face thou art,
> Knocking at heaven with thy brow:
> The worky-daies are the back part;
> The burden of the week lies there,
> Making the whole to stoup and bow,
> Till thy release appeare.

. . . .

Sundaies the pillars are,
On which heav'ns palace arched lies:
The other dayes fill up the spare
And hollow room with vanities.
They are the fruitfull beds and borders
In Gods rich garden: that is bare,
Which parts their ranks and orders.

The Sundaies of mans life,
Thredded together on times string,
Make bracelets to adorn the wife
Of the eternall glorious King.
On Sunday heavens gate stands ope;
Blessings are plentifull and rife,
More plentifull then hope.

The simplicity for which Herbert has been praised (often in contrast to Donne's complexity) is mainly a matter of tone and diction, which is in itself a dramatic device. *The Forerunners* is a good devotional poem, not because 'Thou art still my God' is a simple declaration of faith, but because the statement itself emerges in the context of the speaker's situation and personality successfully realized in the poem; it is embedded in a dramatic poem that employs the devices that are officially rejected. The simple statement is important but its worth and significance are realized only in the context of the poem that gives it full meaning. This is a point worth pursuing. Many of Herbert's best poems of spiritual affirmation show the simple statement of devotion set off in this way. Consider the refrain 'Yet I love thee' in *The Pearl*:

I Know the wayes of Learning; both the head
And pipes that feed the presse, and make it runne;
What reason hath from nature borrowed,
Or of it self, like a good huswife, spunne
In laws and policie; what the starres conspire,
What willing nature speaks, what forc'd by fire;
Both th' old discoveries, and the new-found seas,
The stock and surplus, cause and historie:
All these stand open, or I have the keyes:
Yet I love thee.

I know the wayes of Honour, what maintains
The quick returns of courtesie and wit:
In vies of favours whether partie gains,
When glorie swells the heart, and moldeth it
To all expressions both of hand and eye,
Which on the world a true-love-knot may tie,
And bear the bundle, wheresoe're it goes:
How many drammes of spirit there must be
To sell my life unto my friends or foes:
                    Yet I love thee.

I know the wayes of Pleasure, the sweet strains,
The lullings and the relishes of it;
The propositions of hot bloud and brains;
What mirth and musick mean; what love and wit
Have done these twentie hundred yeares, and more:
I know the project of unbridled store:
My stuffe is flesh, not brasse; my senses live,
And grumble oft, that they have more in me
Then he that curbs them, being but one to five:
                    Yet I love thee.

I know all these, and have them in my hand:
Therefore not sealed, but with open eyes
I flie to thee, and fully understand
Both the main sale, and the commodities;
And at what rate and price I have thy love;
With all the circumstances that may move;
Yet through these labyrinths, not my groveling wit,
But thy silk twist let down from heav'n to me,
Did both conduct and teach me, how by it
                    To climbe to thee.

This is far from the simple formula of *contemptus mundi* or the versified doctrine of 'artless' religious poetry. The reiterated affirmation has its strength largely because the strength of the opposing view, of the worldly attractions, is realized so acutely. The statement of faith is strong too because it is simple, un-explained. The grounds for it are mysterious; it can be justified not by the wisdom of this world but by that higher wisdom which to the reasonable mind seems irrational. It is thus extremely effective dramatically in its placement in the poem, following each detailed explanation of the understandable appeal of the world's attraction in the world's terms with one terse line of 'sweetnesse readie penn'd' that overthrows the whole argument.

One of the best examples of this dramatic use of the simple affirmation is *The Collar*, where the whole deeply realized attraction of the sensual world is overthrown in the final two lines:

> Me thoughts I heard one calling, *Child*!
> And I reply'd, *My Lord*.

If this is the plain 'My God, My King' of the Jordan poems it is also 'good structure in a winding stair'. Another example of the simple declaration of faith, set as an unargued answer to the world's attractions, is appropriately titled *The Quip*:

> The merrie world did on a day
> With his train-bands and mates agree
> To meet together, where I lay,
> And all in sport to geere at me.
>
> First, Beautie crept into a rose,
> Which when I pluckt not, Sir, said she,
> Tell me, I pray, whose hands are those?
> *But thou shalt answer, Lord, for me.*
>
> Then Money came, and chinking still,
> What tune is this, poore man? said he:
> I heard in Musick you had skill.
> *But thou shalt answer, Lord, for me.*
>
> Then came brave Glorie puffing by
> In silks that whistled, who but he?
> He scarce allow'd me half an eie.
> *But thou shalt answer, Lord, for me.*

Then came quick Wit and Conversation,
And he would needs a comfort be,
And, to be short, make an Oration.
But thou shalt answer, Lord, for me.

Yet when the houre of thy designe
To answer these fine things shall come;
Speak not at large; say, I am thine;
And then they have their answer home.

We realize how effective such poems as *The Pearl* and *The Collar* are when we compare them to some less 'artful' rejection of the 'brittle world' such as Southwell's *Lewd Love is Losse*:

Misdeeming eye! that stoopest to the lure
Of mortal worthes, not worth so worthy love;
All beautye's base, all graces are impure,
That do thy erring thoughts from God remove . . .

Base joyes with griefes, bad hopes do end in feares,
Lewd love with losse, evill peace with dedly fighte:
God's love alone doth end with endlesse ease,
Whose joyes in hope, whose hope concludes in peace.[9]

It is the formula, a kind of Christian cliché, that we criticize here, not the sentiment, just as we criticize any poems that are mere formulas and not fully fleshed poems. Such pure religious sentiments may show the 'white sincerity' of the Christian's muse, but their simplicity is not the simplicity of the Herbert poems studied above—even though some such artless purity may be what Herbert yearned for. In these poems we see that Herbert, under the pressure of contrary demands, moves toward a kind of devotional poetry that mediates between these demands in a most fruitful way. The simple love of God exhibits its transcendent value, but only through artistic immersion in the temporal. In this poetry the worth of artless devotion is, through art, dramatized in the complex earthly surroundings that give such devotion a special human meaning and value. By the fullest use of artistic device Herbert contrives to make simplicity poignant; through the literary language 'pure' devotion is placed in its most compelling context.

Occasionally, without agonizing, Herbert seems to recognize something about the place of poetry in his spiritual life that is quite different from the view in the poems cited at the beginning. It is, I think, an insight that is truer to the actual role of his poetry in his relation to God than any of the other views. This is done whimsically in the little poem, *The Quidditie*:

> My God, a verse is not a crown,
> No point of honour, or gay suit,
> No hawk, or banquet, or renown,
> Nor a good sword, nor yet a lute:
>
> It cannot vault, or dance, or play;
> It never was in *France* or *Spain*;
> Nor can it entertain the day;
> With my great stable or demain:
>
> It is no office, art, or news,
> Nor the Exchange, or busie Hall;
> But it is that which while I use
> I am with thee, and *most take all.*

It is revealed more seriously in *Deniall*, where the ability to write poetry and favour with God are closely linked:

> When my devotions could not pierce
>   Thy silent eares;
> Then was my heart broken, as was my verse:
>   My breast was full of fears
>   And disorder:
> . . . .
> Therefore my soul lay out of sight,
>   Untun'd, unstrung:
> My feeble spirit, unable to look right,
>   Like a nipt blossome, hung
>   Discontented.

O cheer and tune my heartlesse breast,
                    Deferre no time;
That so thy favours granting my request,
        They and my minde may chime,
                    And mend my ryme.

Here skill in his art is a manifestation of the ordered soul in tune
with God. It not only brings him close to God, as in *The Quidditie*,
but it is an ordering element in his life and in his relationship with
God. The poem itself figures this wittily in the broken unrhymed
final line of each stanza up to the neat rhyme in the final stanza
which exhibits God mending his poem and his soul's order
simultaneously.

Finally we are led to *The Flower*, the poem so admired by
Coleridge:

How fresh, O Lord, how sweet and clean
Are thy returns! ev'n as the flowers in the spring;
        To which, besides their own demean,
The late-past frosts tributes of pleasure bring.
                    Grief melts away
                    Like snow in May,
As if there were no such cold thing.

Who would have thought my shrivel'd heart
Could have recover'd greennesse? It was gone
        Quite under ground; as flowers depart
To see their mother-root, when they have blown;
                    Where they together
                    All the hard weather,
Dead to the world, keep house unknown.

These are thy wonders, Lord of power,
Killing and quickning, bringing down to hell
        And up to heaven in an houre;
Making a chiming of a passing-bell.
                    We say amisse,
                    This or that is:
Thy word is all, if we could spell.

O that I once past changing were,
Fast in thy Paradise, where no flower can wither!
Many a spring I shoot up fair,
Offring at heav'n, growing and groning thither:
 Nor doth my flower
 Want a spring-showre,
My sinnes and I joining together.

But while I grow in a straight line,
Still upwards bent, as if heav'n were mine own,
Thy anger comes, and I decline:
What frost to that? what pole is not the zone,
 Where all things burn,
 When thou dost turn,
And the least frown of thine is shown?

And now in age I bud again,
After so many deaths I live and write.
I once more smell the dew and rain,
And relish versing: O my onely light
 It cannot be
 That I am he
On whom thy tempests fell all night.

These are thy wonders, Lord of love,
To make us see we are but flowers that glide:
Which when we once can finde and prove,
Thou hast a garden for us, where to bide.
 Who would be more,
 Swelling through store,
Forfeit their Paradise by their pride.

Here we see Herbert, in a moment of deep insight, accepting his 'versing' not only as a part of his earthly 'flowering', with its mortal pride, but perhaps reconciled and accepted to a place in heaven. For his flourishing here, of which his poetry is evidence, pre-figures an abode in the heavenly garden 'where no flower can wither'. The language of poetry is not only the language of earth, but the language of devotion on earth.

These moments are exceptional, however, and the dominant note is that of conflict. Knowing so little of the order of composition of the poems in *The Temple* we cannot say that the point of strain between the requirements of a belief 'clad in simplenesse' and the requirements of an art dressed in 'brave language' was finally relaxed. A reconciliation might have been easier if 'brave' or 'handsome' language meant only sensuous imagery, ornately pictorial expression. This might be easily repudiated. But there is a deeper distrust involved, a suspicion of poetic craftsmanship that extends even to the wit and rhetoric, usually called baroque, stimulated by the Roman church itself in the Counter-Reformation. It is not necessary to draw the line between church and world; it may run right through the church too. In the broad sense of 'classical' Herbert's poetry does reflect intensely one aspect of the tension between the Christian tradition and the classical literary tradition: the opposition between spiritual sincerity and skill in poetry, or, more crudely, between simple truth and contrived art.

NOTES TO CHAPTER III

[1] Citations from Herbert in my text are from *The Works of George Herbert*, ed. F. E. Hutchinson (Oxford, 1941).

[2] *A Divine Centurie of Spirituall Sonnets* (1595), p. 1. Reprinted in *Heliconia*, ed. T. Park (London, 1815), Vol. II.

[3] *The Works of Henry Vaughan*, ed. L. C. Martin (Oxford, 1914), p. 446.

[4] *Ibid*, p. 414.

[5] *John Donne: Complete Poetry and Selected Prose*, ed. John Hayward (Bloomsbury, 1929), p. 276.

[6] *Minor Poets of the Seventeenth Century*, ed. R. G. Howarth (London and New York: Everyman's Library, 1931), p. 140.

[7] *Abraham Cowley: Poems*, ed. A. R. Waller (Cambridge, 1905), p. 12f.

[8] Cited by Hutchinson, Herbert's *Works*, p. 495.

[9] *The Complete Poems of Robert Southwell*, ed. Alexander B. Grosart (London, 1872), p. 90.

CHAPTER IV

Marvell
A New Pastoralism

No POEM better exhibits the tension between Christian and classical traditions, or is more profitably studied with an understanding of that tension, than Andrew Marvell's *The Coronet*. It is a poem built on the contrast of crowns, a contrast that is also given considerable symbolic weight by Donne and Carew. Donne's *La Corona*, mentioned earlier, is a nice gauge of the values involved in the contrast:

> But doe not, with a vile crowne of fraile bayes,
> Reward my muses white sincerity,
> But what thy thorny crowne gain'd, that give mee,
> A crowne of Glory, which doth flower alwayes.[1]

On the Christian side is the crown of thorns, which prefigures the crown of glory, an emblem of the victory over sin on 'the dry, leafless trunk on Golgotha', a victory of Christ's truth 'clad with simplenesse'. On the pagan side is the laureate crown, or crown of bays, or the flowery garland of the erotic pastoral, an emblem of the sensual world realized and exploited by literary art. Marvell begins with the crown of thorns:

> When for the Thorns with which I long, too long,
>   With many a piercing wound,
>   My Saviours head have crown'd,
> I seek with Garlands to redress that Wrong:
>   Through every Garden, every Mead,
> I gather flow'rs(my fruits are only flow'rs)

Dismantling all the fragrant Towers
That once adorn'd my Shepherdesses head.[2]

The sinner recrucifies Christ every day. Marvell's particular sins
are seen as thorns added to Christ's crown of thorns, a wrong that
it would seem appropriate to redress 'with Garlands'. Both the sin
and the redress refer to the public matter of his poetry, for Marvell
is here speaking in the role of a poet and not of any private guilt.
What are the poetic sins against the Saviour? They are what nearly
every seventeenth-century poet felt guilty about, 'idle verse',
specifically secular love poetry praising a mistress and celebrating
the natural world. As Southwell has it:

> Christ's thorne is sharpe, no head His garland weares;
> Stil finest wits are 'stilling Venus' rose,
> In Paynim toyes the sweetest vaines are spent.[3]

Each poem in this tradition is a thorn adding 'a piercing wound' to
Christ's head. To redress this wrong 'with Garlands' will be to
make poems honouring Christ instead of the mistress usually glori-
fied. The garland of flowers is a traditional token for the lover in
the erotic pastoral; for the poet-lover, the song of praise itself
may be emblematic of that garland. The May Queen receives
such garlands. The garland, as a mark of distinction, also suggests
the Greek or Roman wreath conferred to honour achievement.
A further meaning of garland as 'a collection of short literary
pieces' (*NED* 4. fig.) is also properly read here.

Gathering flowers for this garland is, first, to do what was done
for the pastoral lover, in fact, to convert those flowers adorning
her into an adornment for Christ. In the search 'through every
Garden, every Mead' we remember how intimately flowering
nature is associated with the lover's world, particularly in the
pastoral. The beauties of nature are now to be turned to a new use.
Gathering flowers is also, however, to be read as the assembling of
a poem, collecting beauties, 'dismantling' the former poetry for
new use. Marvell adds, in an illuminating aside, that 'my fruits are
only flow'rs'. They are merely beautiful. This applies directly to

the poetry. He has dealt with lovely things, but loveliness without further yield, frail beauty without fruitful end—in other words, a purely aesthetic or hedonistic world. Marvell here reveals a primary complaint against imaginative literary art in the classical tradition: its apparent lack of moral and spiritual substance—the absence, that is to say, of truth as Christians know it. 'By their fruits ye shall know them', and his fruits are only flowers.

> And now when I have summ'd up all my store,
>   Thinking (so I my self deceive)
>   So rich a Chaplet thence to weave
> As never yet the king of Glory wore:
>   Alas I find the Serpent old
>   That, twining in his speckled breast,
>   About the flow'rs disguis'd does fold,
>   With wreaths of Fame and Interest.

The weaving of the rich Chaplet of the gathered flowers is the making of the poem honouring Christ. Such a conception of the careful composition of the poem is consistent with the tradition from which such a poem would come. It is the conception of the poetic craftsman that George Herbert found so hard to reconcile with his idea of spiritual sincerity, of the poet as the unselfconscious vessel of God's truth or reflector of God's glory. Uncovered here is a point of high tension between Christian and classical attitudes toward the poet.

We may distinguish in this conflict two main conceptions of the role of the poet, both present in the classical period, to be sure, but raised through the Christian viewpoint to a kind of crisis in the period under consideration. One is the conception of the poet as a maker, a craftsman in imaginative art—the poet visualized, for example, in the *Ars Poetica*. The other is the conception of the poet as a prophet, the spontaneous 'oracle' possessed by the spirit that delivers a message through him. The latter, Plato's conception,[4] is, like so much of Plato, very congenial to the Christian position. It represents what Herbert, when he reasoned like a philosopher, wanted to be, copying out a 'sweetnesse readie penn'd'. It is congenial because of the emphasis on the 'truth' that gets through, the faith in the Word that brings into the world the abstractions known by the Reason. The poet, poor vessel, is seized by it, subordinate to it. The former conception, that of the craftsman, is, by its nature, irrevocably at odds with this conception. The poet contrives his poem with wit, invention, fancy, imaginations, etc. (to use later terms), and is likely to exercise these faculties on, or through, the material of concrete experience, the immediately felt world. It might be expected that this conception, combined with the so-called 'pagan spirit' in the celebration of sensual nature, would inevitably clash with the 'revived spirit of the Early Church'. Profound and age-old critical viewpoints are engaged here, as we know, though we are concerned now with only one manifestation of that conflict.

Now when the flowers are gathered, i.e. when the poet has assembled the beauties of nature with which he deals, and which are associated with his sensual world, the fatal defect is discovered: he finds the Serpent disguised in the flowers, his original lair. Here is Satan tempting a repetition of the original sensual fault, working in the 'natural' world in the sense that he wins man through a victory by man's animal nature over his 'higher' powers of reason, the faculties imaging God and the heavenly powers. The poet thus debases 'Heaven's Diadem' with the remains of fallen nature:

> Ah, foolish Man, that would'st debase with them
> And mortal Glory, Heaven's Diadem!

The poet cannot redress the wrong in the usual way of poetry for he repeats the original offence and seemingly recrowns Christ with thorns.

> But thou who only could'st the Serpent tame,
> Either his slipp'ry knots at once untie,
> And disintangle all his winding Snare:
> Or shatter too with him my curious frame
> And let these wither, so that he may die,
> Though set with Skill and chosen out with Care.
> That they, while Thou on both their Spoils dost tread,
> May crown thy Feet, that could not crown thy Head.

The poet appeals to Christ to separate nature from sin, get Satan out of it (and, figuratively, get Satan out of poetry). Viewed this way, nature is not in itself evil, but is a victim, as man is a victim. Remove Satan and it will return to its unfallen innocence. Or, if nature and sin are inseparable then, it occurs to the poet, here is the possibility of presenting a real crown, a crown appropriate for Christ. He invites Christ to smite Satan through him, sacrificing himself, as a poet, and the flowers. To get at Satan, to deprive him of his hiding place, shatter the 'curious frame' (the elaborately wrought chaplet, i.e. the poem) and let the flowers wither; the poet will give up natural beauty 'though set with Skill and chosen out with Care'. 'Skill' and 'Care' have a clear application to the theory of poetry mentioned above, to the kind of artful composition that made the first unacceptable garland. The resultant crowning of Christ's feet is a sacrifice, and a proper penance for the adding of thorns to Christ's head—where the garland was not.

The crowning of Christ's feet is an act of humility and repentance. We are bound to think of Mary Magdalen here, washing Christ's feet with her hair. The association is apt, for it is particularly suggestive of penitence for sensual fault. Furthermore, it is performed with the very emblems of former sensual experience, Magdalen's hair and Marvell's garland of flowers. That Marvell conceived of the Magdalen this way we know fron *Eyes and Tears*:

> So Magdalen, in Tears mor wise
> Dissolv'd those captivating Eyes,
> Whose liquid Chaines could flowing meet
> To fetter her Redeemers feet.

Mary Magdalen is, in fact, generally identified with the mistress of love poetry, come to reform. Vaughan makes her a lady of courtly love:

> This dusky state of sighs and tears
> Durst not look on those smiling years,
> When Magdal-castle was thy seat,
> Where all was sumptuous, rare and neat.

He describes her hair when she 'then did dress the much-lov'd toy/ In Spires, Globes, angry Curls and coy', and makes the common additional contrast of the penitential weeping with the lover's tears:

> Learn, Ladies, here the faithful cure
> Makes beauty lasting, fresh, and pure;
> Learn Marys art of tears, and then
> Say, *You have got the day from men.*
> Cheap, mighty Art! her Art of love
> Who lov'd much, and much more could move . . .
> Her Art! whose pensive, weeping eyes,
> Were once sins loose and tempting spies;
> But now are fixed stars, whose light
> Helps such dark straglers to their sight.[5]

The Coronet is thus a Christian poem of penitence, treating the peculiar kind of penitence proper to a poet's sins. It involves an effort directed against much that we consider central in the classical literary tradition. *Clorinda and Damon* is another poem that works in the same direction, though in this case within the classical form and in the classical setting itself. Clorinda and Damon are the nymph and shepherd of an ostensibly erotic pastoral; the poem is the dialogue between them, a common device to present the suit of the lover, his arguments, the beginning refusals and coquetry of the nymph, the final victory. Here it is the nymph who makes the original invitation:

> *C.* Damon come drive thy flocks this way.
> *D.* No: 'tis too late they went astray.
> *C.* I have a grassy Scutcheon spy'd,
>   Where Flora blazons all her pride.
> The Grass I aim to feast thy Sheep:
> The Flow'rs I for thy Temples keep.

But Damon's answer is surprising: 'Grass withers; and the Flow'rs too fade.' Clorinda makes the *carpe diem* argument:

> C. Seize the short Joyes then, ere they vade.
>   Seest thou that unfrequented Cave?
> D. That den? C. Loves Shrine. D. But Virtue's Grave.
> C. In whose cool bosome we may lye
>   Safe from the Sun. D. not Heaven's Eye.

This is clearly no way for a swain to talk. Clorinda is still a pagan nymph, offering the standard enticements of nature, but something has happened to Damon; he realizes he has a soul and he is concerned for it. Their dialogue is becoming a debate between soul and sense.

> C. Near this, a Fountaines liquid Bell
>   Tinkles within a concave Shell.
> D. Might a Soul bath there and be clean,
>   Or slake its Drought? C. What is't you mean?
> D. These once had been enticing things,
>   Clorinda, Pastures, Caves, and Springs.
> C. And what late change? D. The other day
>   Pan met me. C. What did great Pan say?
> D. Words that transcend poor Shepherds skill,
>   But He ere since my Songs does fill:
>   And his Name swells my slender Oate.

Pan is Christ, an identification that was easy to make considering the common false etymology of 'pan' (all), which, applied to the god, gave him a metaphysical significance that allowed an association with the Creator.[6] This association is further supported by the conception of Christ as the Good Shepherd. The poem concludes with a hymn to Pan as Christ:

> C. Sweet must Pan sound in Damons Note.
> D. Clorinda's voice might make it sweet.
> C. Who would not in Pan's Praises meet?
>   Chorus.
>   Of Pan the flowry Pastures sing,
>   Caves eccho, and the Fountains ring.
>   Sing then while he doth us inspire;
>   For all the World is our Pan's Quire.

The 'Pastures, Caves, and Springs' of nature that had before been the enticements and supports of sensual love, now sing their Creator in what we can presume is a hymn of heavenly rather than earthly love. Instead of retiring to the grotto to make garlands for each other, the pair join in the choir singing Pan's praises. Christ has entered the world of the swains and nymphs, and they learn that they have souls. So the pastoral spree is ended and the pastoral song is transformed. An important thing to notice here is how the pastoral serves as a meeting-ground for the two traditions. In explaining this we recognize that there is both a Biblical pastoralism and a classical pastoralism. It is easy and natural for a poet to mix them, as we see in the identification of Pan and Christ above. A particularly inviting opportunity to associate them appears in the Nativity story, in which the shepherds are frequently treated as swains of the classical pastoral. Milton does this in his Nativity ode:

> The Shepherds on the Lawn,
> Or ere the point of dawn,
>   Sate simply chatting in a rustick row;
> Full little thought they than,
> That the mighty Pan
>   Was kindly come to live with them below;
> Perhaps their loves, or else their sheep,
> Was all that did their silly thoughts so busie keep. [7]

Crashaw's shepherds are named Tityrus and Thyrsis in *A Hymne of the Nativity, sung by the Shepheards.* They are

>   poore Shepheards, simple things,
>   That use no varnish, no oyl'd Arts,
>   But lift clean hands full of cleare hearts. [8]

This indicates clearly the point of contact between the two traditions. It is the natural innocence of the pastoral world in the classical tradition that permits the association with Biblical pastoralism. Each tradition has its own kind of pastoralism, but the poets here make a deliberate confusion of the two, a strategy that works to fuse and reconcile the traditions. The outstanding example of this fusion, of course, is *Lycidas*, where the shepherd is both pastoral poet and Christian pastor.

The Christianity that has come to Marvell's pastoral world appears in *A Dialogue between Thyrsis and Dorinda*. Here the shepherd tells his nymph of heaven, which is a combination of the Elysian Fields and the Christian Paradise. He knows it requires 'a Chast Soul' to get there and that there is heard the 'Musick of the Spheares', but for the most part it is a shepherd's Elysium with the fattest sheep, prettiest flowers, and no wolves or cold winds, where 'every Nimph's a Queen of May'. What is interesting is the child-like approach to it all, a primitivism that has been touched somewhat by the Christian scheme but hardly at all by the spirit behind it. The pair are, in a way, still 'innocent' of Christianity.

In these poems the emphasis is clearly Christian. In the first two poems a Christian position is taken against the two main characteristics of secular love poetry in the classical tradition: (1) its artfulness, or insincerity, (2) its immersion in the sensual aspects of nature. Whereas the former was a principal source of conflict in Herbert, the latter is of paramount interest in Marvell. His reaction, however, is not nearly as clearcut as Herbert's. To speak of nature in Marvell is to strike into the core of his best poems. I do not mean by this that nature is a constant, fixed symbol or quantity throughout Marvell's poetry. It is not, though by selective quotation we may make it seem so. What I propose here is merely an examination of an important aspect of nature as it recurs in Marvell's poems, a selection relevant to the issue raised above. This is also an examination of Marvell's pastoralism, for nature is a prime support of the pastoral perspective.

We may begin by reviewing the conception of nature in *The Coronet*. There the flowers, and all they stood for, were tainted, unfit for the crown. But they were not originally or innately unfit. Nature did not seem in itself evil, but, like man, had been victimized by Satan, who used nature for his hiding place. This may seem a small qualification, but it is not often made by Christian poets rejecting the world and the flesh. At one point the speaker evinced a hope to disentangle Satan from nature and return it to its unfallen innocence. It will be well to keep this in mind as we approach the other poems.

First should be mentioned two poems that are unmistakably Christian in outlook, *A Dialogue Between the Resolved Soul and Created Pleasure*, and *On a Drop of Dew*. In the first the soul opposes the five senses and answers victoriously the inducements of each. The chorus comments:

> Earth cannot shew so brave a Sight
> As when a single Soul does fence
> The Batteries of alluring Sense.

Next are offered female beauty, gold, glory, and knowledge. All temptations are answered perfectly. *On a Drop of Dew* is a sensuous and conceited formulation of the relation of the Christian soul to the world of sense, of nature, which it shuns.

Yet the nature of both these poems is not the nature of Comus, the nature that by animal example excuses licence and urges appetite. This does not make its allurement less dangerous to the soul, but it puts the potential evil more in the soul's approach to nature than in nature itself. Nature in Marvell is never vile, only secondary. Says the soul, 'Had I but any time to lose,/On this I would it all dispose.' When nature's scattered beauty is concentrated in one supreme manifestation, female beauty, the soul answers, 'If things of Sight such Heavens be,/What Heavens are those we cannot see?' The poet may here find some justification in showing what Heavens there are in things of sight. For, when these are rejected, we have a strong index of the attraction of the world that shuns them, that makes them secondary. This is what happens in *On a Drop of Dew*, which does full justice to the world of natural beauty. In the single fundamental metaphor on which the poem is built, the drop of dew figuring the soul, the vehicle, the dew-drop, is exploited lovingly for all its natural beauty, 'Shed from the Bosom of the Morn/Into the blowing Roses,' at the same time that it yearns for its home in the sky. The soul that slights the world slights a sweet world:

> So the Soul, that Drop, that Ray
> Of the clear Fountain of Eternal Day
> Could it within the humane flow'r be seen,
>   Remembring still its former height,
>   Shuns the sweet leaves and blossoms green;
>   And, recollecting its own Light,
> Does, in its pure and circling thoughts, express
> The greater Heaven in an Heaven less.

A Dialogue between the Soul and Body varies a customary Christian viewpoint. In the traditional Christian debate between soul and body, the body, as might be expected, plays a part that can only be described as that of the straight man. That is, the body has no real argument but sets up claims for the carnal life that are completely overwhelmed from the side of the angels. The most interesting characteristic of Marvell's poem is the strong argument advanced by the body. After the soul introduces the usual complaint of being the prisoner of the inferior body, 'hung up, as 'twere; in Chains/Of Nerves, and Arteries, and Veins', the body makes an interesting retort:

> O who shall me deliver whole,
> From bonds of this Tyrannic Soul?
> Which strecht upright, impales me so,
> That mine own Precipice I go;
> And warms and moves this needless Frame:
> (A Fever could but do the same.)
> And, wanting where its spight to try,
> Has made me live to let me dye.
> A body that could never rest,
> Since this ill Spirit it possest.

This is not quite legitimate. The body is taking 'soul' here in the original broad meaning: the characteristic of life, the principle by which a thing is alive. To the soul's further complaint against imprisonment and sensory pain the body replies:

> But Physick yet could never reach
> The Maladies Thou me dost teach;

> Whom first the Cramp of Hope does Tear:
> And then the Palsie Shakes of Fear.
> The Pestilence of Love does heat:
> Or Hatred's hidden Ulcer eat.
> Joy's chearful Madness does perplex:
> Or Sorrow's other Madness vex.
> Which Knowledge forces me to know;
> And Memory will not foregoe.

This blames the passions on the soul, all of which disturb the originally happy vegetable life of the body. The body has the last word, and it is a most telling one:

> What but a Soul could have the wit
> To build me up for Sin so fit?
> So Architects do square and hew,
> Green Trees that in the Forest grew.

This makes the soul responsible for sin. In its natural state the body was as innocent as a plant; only when it is given a soul is it seasoned for sin. The final image conveys the idea that the body's natural condition, like the green trees in the forest, is its proper one. Yet the image does not work entirely for the body. Architects don't ruin the tree. Only when they try to make something of the tree is it liable to these defects; only when God makes something of the body, giving it a soul, is it liable to sin. Be that as it may, the characteristic Marvell idea here is the conception of a bodily or natural innocence, an almost pre-Christian condition that has its virtues too. We can call this a pastoral perspective insofar as it uses a wise conception of the natural against more sophisticated ideas, in this case the Christian concern for the soul.

This bodily innocence points, then, to a conception of the natural that, to some extent, works *against* the religious tradition. It does not follow that it works *for* the erotic tradition. For Marvell's nature stands against the erotic tradition too, as we see in the Mower poems. In *The Mower against Gardens*, the Mower, a pastoral figure, objects to what man has made of nature in the civilized garden; all the fertilizing, cultivating, and grafting has produced something unnatural and unwholesome. The terms employed suggest the seduction of rustic woman into a sophisticated and artificially heightened sensuality:

> Luxurious Man, to bring his Vice in use,
>   Did after him the World seduce:
> And from the fields the Flow'rs and Plants allure
>   Where Nature was most plain and pure.
> He first enclos'd within the Gardens square
>   A dead and standing pool of Air:
> And a more luscious Earth for them did knead,
>   Which stupifi'd them while it fed.

The flowers then appear as artful women:

> With strange perfumes he did the Roses taint
> And Flow'rs themselves were taught to paint.
> The tulip, white, did for complexion seek;
>   And learn'd to interline its cheek.

These suggestions become more pronounced until finally the whole process is viewed in sexual terms, a decadent and eventually sterile sensuality:

> And yet these Rarities might be allow'd,
>   To Man, that sov'raign thing and proud;
>   Had he not dealt between the Bark and Tree,
>   Forbidden mixtures there to see.
> No Plant now knew the Stock from which it came;
>   He grafts upon the Wild the Tame;
> That the uncertain and adult'rate fruit
>   Might put the Palate in dispute.
> His green Seraglio has its Eunuchs too;
>   Lest any Tyrant him out-doe.
> And in the Cherry he does Nature vex,
>   To procreate without a Sex.

The climactic line makes clear the difference between the quality of nature so employed by man and nature's original quality:

'Tis all enforc'd; the Fountain and the Grot;
While the sweet Fields do lye forgot:
Where willing nature does to all dispence
A wild and fragrant Innocence.

Marvell's nature here takes on special interest when we remember the long support fertile nature lent to the erotic argument, particularly in the erotic pastoral, serving as permissive background, as justification for animal impulse, as example of the fleeting pleasure to be seized. It is the support always available to one, like Comus, making a case against chastity: 'Wherefore did nature pour her bounties forth/ . . . But all to please, and sate the curious taste?' (*Comus*, 710–4). Marvell uses nature this way on occasion, to be sure, but his nature revealed in the above poem is far more subtle. In the use of nature in the typical erotic lyric, nature seems to sanction a sensuality free from the sense of sin, a primitivism that implies a kind of pre-Christian or pre-moral state. Christ has not yet arrived among the shepherds to tell them that they have a soul. Marvell's nature implies an even greater innocence; it is almost pre-sexual. Not that it is not sensual. It is a world of natural delight, certainly. But it has not yet been deflowered, so to speak. This is meant seriously, for there is, as has often been pointed out, an intimate connection between Marvell's garden and virginity. Again and again unspoiled nature appears as the haven of chastity. In *The Picture of little T. C. in a Prospect of Flowers*, for example, the garden nurtures the chaste young soul who must later enter combat with 'wanton Love'. In *The Nymph Complaining for the death of her Faun* the fawn, representing innocence in the garden, becomes a patron and symbol of chastity. Nature conceived in this way may be used not only against the religious tradition but against the erotic tradition too.

In *The Mower to the Glo-Worms* the glow-worms preside over a diminutive and innocuous world. They are lamps that let the nightingale read her music, comets that bode no real harm:

Ye Country Comets, that portend
No War, nor Princes funeral,

> Shining unto no higher end
> Than to presage the Grasses fall;

This is uninvaded nature, and the Mower is part of it in a serious sense. The glow-worms show the Mower his way, his physical path:

> Ye Glo-worms, whose officious Flame
> To wandring Mowers shows the way,
> That in the Night have lost their aim,
> And after foolish Fires do stray;

But bringing the Mower back from 'foolish fires' (the term echoes the moral judgment of the *ignis fatuus*) is to do more than give him his physical bearings; it is to guide him in his way of life which, I take it, is properly one with the glow-worms and nightingales. But we learn in the last stanza that a 'foolish fire' has thrown the Mower irretrievably off course and that nature *has* been invaded: a woman has arrived and deranged the simple Mower:

> Your courteous Lights in vain you wast,
> Since Juliana here is come,
> For She my Mind hath so displac'd
> That I shall never find my home.

The poem is, of course, a compliment to Juliana, a tribute to the power of her charms. If this were not Marvell, and we were not alert to his characteristic concerns, we might let it go at that. But, on the other hand, it is not a mere exercise of ingenuity to see more in the poem, and use it to clarify Marvell's conception of nature. Or, to put it the other way around, we can use what we already know of Marvell's conception of nature to illuminate the full significance of the poem. It works both ways.

The Mower's Song is the same kind of compliment, and it reveals the same rather reproachful suggestion that the woman is the 'spoiler' in nature, introducing a new delight that is not under control, not innocuous, not compatible with the order nature exhibits when it is uncharged with sex.

My Mind was once the true survey
Of all these Medows fresh and gay;
And in the greenness of the Grass
Did see its Hopes as in a Glass;
When Juliana came, and She
What I do to the Grass, does to my Thoughts and Me.

As in the poem to the glow-worms, the Mower is a member of
the green society, though the influence of the woman has deprived
him of his place:

Unthankful Medows, could you so
A fellowship so true forego,
And in your gawdy May-games meet,
While I lay trodden under feet?
When Juliana came, and She
What I do to the Grass, does to my Thoughts and Me.

But what you in Compassion ought,
Shall now by my revenge be wrought:
And Flow'rs, and Grass, and I and all,
Will in one common Ruine fall.
For Juliana comes, and She
What I do to the Grass, does to my Thoughts and Me.

The Mower will fall to Juliana and he will make the flowers and
grass fall with him. We cannot miss the parallel suggested by the
language here. Nature and the man 'will in one common Ruine
fall./For Juliana comes'. 'Ruine' is too strong for the conventional
upsets of love; it applies to the fall in the original garden. Pleasure
in nature and the balance in the mind are lost with the coming of
the woman. Here it is a nymph affecting a swain, hardly a disaster
ordinarily, and quite proper to the goings-on in the Arcadian
Golden Age. Marvell, however, puts the Golden Age back one
remove to a time of natural innocence that is not only innocent
of sin, but innocent of sex. He takes a pastoral view that, by an
extra step, brings the usual pastoral view itself under criticism.

Once we recognize the parallel to the original fall we sense the continued serious undertones in the last stanza. The poem is still a testimonial to the power of the woman's charms, and the lover dying for love may be seen as part of the hyperbolic compliment:

> And thus, ye Meadows, which have been
> Companions of my thoughts more green,
> Shall now the Heraldry become
> With which I shall adorn my Tomb;
> For Juliana comes, and She
> What I do to the Grass, does to my Thoughts and Me.

But the meadows' companionship and the green thoughts have too much symbolic weight by now to appear insignificantly. This stanza too takes up the consequence of a fall in its more serious aspect, the transformation in the 'common Ruine'. For the man it is death; the earth becomes his tomb. And flowering nature, now fallen, only adorns a tomb.

We have, to recapitulate, observed in the classical-erotic tradition a widespread use of nature set as the permissive background of erotic sport. But Marvell, using the very form and outer machinery of the erotic pastoral, is here using nature against the erotic tradition. It is not a moralizing or otherworldly comment he makes, but a comment from within the natural, sensual world itself, asserting the claim of a purer delight. It is not the vacant innocence of the ascetic, though it does nurture the contemplative and rested mind in withdrawal. The innocence is not an emasculated innocence but 'a wild and fragrant innocence'. In its wild aspects, however, it is not the opposite of the holy, nor in its innocent aspects is it the opposite of the sensual.

This last point is illustrated most clearly in *The Garden*, which certainly betokens a sensual delight:

> No white nor red was ever seen
> So am'rous as this lovely green . . .
> . . . .
> What wond'rous Life is this I lead!
> Ripe Apples drop about my head;
> The Luscious Clusters of the Vine

> Upon my mouth do crush their Wine;
> The Nectaren, and curious Peach,
> Into my hands themselves do reach;
> Stumbling on Melons, as I pass,
> Insnar'd with Flow'rs, I fall on Grass.

Yet it is an innocuous sensuality. Its difference from other snares and falls in the Garden of Adam and Eve is seen in the harmless result of its fecundity, a teasingly suggestive comparison to the other fall: 'Stumbling on Melons as I pass/Insnar'd with Flow'rs, I fall on Grass.' At the same time, this kind of sensual nature is the support and background, not of sexual licence, but of the harmonious activity of the mind in peaceful withdrawal from unnatural disturbance:

> . . . all Flow'rs and all Trees do close
> To weave the Garlands of repose.

> Fair quiet, have I found thee here,
> And Innocence thy Sister dear!

> Your sacred Plants, if here below,
> Only among the Plants will grow.

There is no suggestion here of the rule of instinct and spontaneous passion, justified by identification with animal creation. Instead, the mind and soul are harmoniously at their best, balanced and at home in their proper surroundings.

> Mean while the Mind, from pleasure less,
> Withdraws into its happiness:
> The Mind, that Ocean where each kind
> Does streight its own resemblance find;
> Yet it creates, transcending these,
> Far other Worlds, and other Seas;
> Annihilating all that's made
> To a green Thought in a green Shade.

It is hard to go outside of Marvell's terms here, particularly when we approach the celebrated closing couplet of the stanza. The transcendental greenery of the imagination is apparently the supreme achievement in the green world of the garden; it both reflects the essential qualities of the garden, and itself formulates the garden, giving it an over-arching meaning and significance in man's whole apprehension of the world. A mind in such a situation, working on such material, provides a kind of molten identification of the two, mind and nature, translating the natural and material world to a higher realm of existence, while the imagination in turn is figured in that world.

The soul is more purely soul, 'Casting the Bodies Vest aside.' But even this, though it seems to be a movement away from the earthly, appears in an image so sensuous that here too there seems to be an identification of the lovely garden state with the character of the soul:

> Here at the Fountains sliding foot,
> Or at some Fruit-trees mossy root,
> Casting the Bodies Vest aside,
> My soul into the boughs does glide:
> There like a Bird it sits, and sings,
> Then whets, and combs its silver Wings;
> And, till prepar'd for longer flight,
> Waves in its Plumes the various Light.

That this is the pre-sexual garden we realize in the eighth stanza, and may connect nature here with the nature of the Mower poems:

> Such was that happy Garden-state,
> While Man there walk'd without a Mate:
> After a Place so pure, and sweet,
> What other Help could yet be meet!
> But 'twas beyond a Mortal's share
> To wander solitary there:
> Two Paradises 'twere in one
> To live in Paradise alone.

Our final view must be that Marvell's nature comes to embody values that are neither wholly in the religious tradition nor wholly in the erotic tradition. His 'nature' is, in fact, defined against certain conceptions of nature in each tradition. Marvell's is a very special kind of pastoralism. He seems to carry the natural innocence of classical pastoralism, which so often supported a sinless sexuality, a step further into a yet more primitive state, a pre-sexual or non-sexual innocence (like that of Eden before the coming of Eve) that nourishes the mind and resembles the philosophical, or religious, retreat from the world, yet which responds fully to the natural world in a kind of intense but unspecified sensuality of the whole being. From this 'pastoral' perspective he is able to regard both the erotic and the ascetic traditions as departures from a natural, 'primitive', and healthy human norm.

All this does not make for a simple meaning, and in this Marvell's poetry is certainly more complex in symbolic import than that of any other metaphysical poet. His use of nature, balanced, as it were, between the two traditions, accounts in great part for this depth.

NOTES TO CHAPTER IV

[1] *John Donne: Complete Poetry and Selected Prose*, ed. John Hayward (Bloomsbury, 1929), p. 276.

[2] Citations from Marvell in my text are to *The Poems and Letters of Andrew Marvell*, ed. H. M. Margoliouth, 2 vols. (Oxford, 1927).

[3] Second prefatory poem, 'The Author to the Reader', *The Complete Poems of Robert Southwell*, ed. Alexander B. Grosart (London, 1872).

[4] See *Ion*, 234.

[5] 'St Mary Magdalen', *The Works of Henry Vaughan*, ed. L. C. Martin (Oxford, 1914), II, 507.

[6] Exhibited by Spenser, for example, in the glosse to *Maye*: 'The Name is most rightly . . . applied to him, for Pan signifieth all, or omnipotent, which is onely the Lord Jesus.' Merritt Y. Hughes calls attention to this in connection with Milton's identification of Pan and Christ in the Nativity ode. See *Paradise Regained, the Minor Poems, and Samson Agonistes*, ed. Merritt Y. Hughes (New York, 1937), p. 156n.

[7] *The Works of John Milton* (New York, 1931–9), the Columbia Milton, I, part I, p. 4.

[8] *The Poems . . . of Richard Crashaw*, ed. L. C. Martin (Oxford, 1927), p. 108.

CHAPTER V

Milton

I

IF THE relation of classical and Christian traditions is worth our attention in the poets just considered, how much might we expect to find in Milton, whose modes stand so clearly in the classical tradition and whose subjects and purposes are so seriously Christian. Indeed the issue has so many sides in Milton's poetry that it will be a good idea, in the beginning, to distinguish the present approach from others that are possible.

If we consider only the mere mixture of classical and Christian reference in Milton's poetry, we find that nearly all of the important poems exhibit a mingling of the two traditions, raw material potentially evocative of the tension that is our main concern. This mingling is, of course, not peculiar to Milton, nor is it necessarily evocative of tension, but it is worth noting and it could be documented at length. An exhaustive study of the matter would take into account, for example, such interesting blends as, in *On the Morning of Christ's Nativity*, the portrayal of the Hebrew shepherds as the shepherds of the classical pastoral and, particularly the identification of Pan with Christ, as noted earlier:[1]

> The Shepherds on the Lawn,
> Or ere the point of dawn,
>   Sate simply chatting in a rustick row;
> Full little thought they than,
> That the mighty *Pan*
>   Was kindly come to live with them below;
> Perhaps their loves, or else their sheep,
> Was all that did their silly thoughts so busie keep.[2]

104

It would be easy, I suppose, to make too much of this as an important 'fusion' of the two traditions. There is always the question of how far any mixture is a significant fusion of classical and Christian and how far it is merely part of the characteristic Renaissance effort, even mania, to give everything the elegance of the classical term. Certainly there are all degrees of significance possible in these blends. The fusion here, I take it, is smooth, uncomplicated, hardly fundamental to the theme—a graceful satisfaction of 'literary' expectations in a religious poem—but it goes some distance beyond mere literary swank. *Lycidas*, however, in both its form and its imagery, provides a more exciting combination of the two traditions. A full study would concentrate there, I think, on the character of the shepherd as the poet-priest, and particularly on his identification with Orpheus.[3] In *Comus* the use of classical machinery and image as a vehicle for Christian ideas would merit attention.

It would be possible to dwell at length on the varying relations of these elements in each poem; however, I here propose to attend fully only to *Paradise Lost*—where the issue is of surpassing interest—and merely observe that the mingling of the traditions, with which the tension begins, is clear and abundant in Milton's poetry. I should also, before turning to *Paradise Lost*, observe that Milton was well aware of the conflict between these traditions, as is apparent in the well-known rejection of classical learning and art by Christ in *Paradise Regained*. We remember what is said of classical literature there:

> Or if I would delight my private hours
> With Music or with Poem, where so soon
> As in our native Language can I find
> That solace? All our Law and Story strew'd
> With Hymns, our Psalms with artful terms inscrib'd,
> Our Hebrew Songs and Harps in Babylon,
> That pleas'd so well our Victors ear, declare
> That rather Greece from us these Arts deriv'd;
> Ill imitated, while they loudest sing
> The vices of thir Deities, and thir own
> In Fable, Hymn, or Song, so personating

Thir Gods ridiculous, and themselves past shame.
Remove their swelling Epithets thick laid
As varnish on a Harlots cheek, the rest,
Thin sown with aught of profit or delight,
Will far be found unworthy to compare
With Sion's songs, to all true tasts excelling,
Where God is prais'd aright, and Godlike men,
The Holiest of Holies, and his Saints.

(IV, 331–49)

If we look at *Paradise Lost* as a classical poem only in respect to its mythological reference we find evidence of Milton's uneasiness in his use of classical material there, too. A case in point is the transformation of Urania, the goddess of the heavens, into the Christian Heavenly Muse. It has often been cited as a characteristic and successful accommodation of the pagan to the Christian. Though the transformation is certainly accomplished without much strain, we cannot help noticing the scrupulous care Milton takes to strip his Urania of her pagan garb. In the invocation to Book VII he is using only the *name* Urania (' . . . by that name/ If rightly thou art called. . . . The meaning, not the Name I call . . .') for the mystical voice of Christian inspiration; he makes sure we know it is not really Urania, though he takes advantage of the literary associations connected with the classical Muse and the kind of poet she inspires. *His* inspiration is comparable in its kind, but incomparably superior in its effect. It is real and true, from the Fountain of Light, not fabled and false. Her care is better than that of the Muse who could not defend Orpheus: 'So fail not thou, who thee implores:/For thou art Heav'nlie, shee an empty dreame.' The simultaneous comparison with, and diminution of, the classical equivalent is Milton's characteristic way of handling such material. This is consistent with his attitude toward his whole project in its relation to his literary models. His son 'intends to soar/Above the Aonian Mount' (I, 14f.) and 'above the Olympian Hill' (VII, 3). His argument is 'Not less but more Heroic then the wrauth/Of stern Achilles . . .' (IX, 14f.).

If we reckon all the plain classical material that gets into the poem as embellishment and ask how it normally appears, we find

106

that, though it contributes its effect, it is nearly always qualified or negated with the same care exhibited in the handling of Urania. Such a procedure is necessary, apparently, because the official subject of the poem is entirely Christian. The narrative is true, the Word of God. Classical myth, on the other hand, is false and the Christian poet cannot appear to give credence to it. The lovely Mulciber passage is typical, bracketed as it is with the clear disclaimers 'they fabl'd' and 'thus they relate,/Erring':

> Men call'd him Mulciber; and how he fell
> From Heav'n, they fabl'd, thrown by angry Jove
> Sheer o're the Chrystal Battlements: from Morn
> To Noon he fell, from Noon to dewy Eve,
> A Summers day; and with the setting Sun
> Dropt from the Zenith like a falling Star,
> On Lemnos th' Aegean Ile: thus they relate,
> Erring . . .
>
> (I, 740–7)

The simultaneous likening to, and decrement of, the classical analogue usually includes the conscientious note that the classical is but 'feign'd', a word that appears again and again. Eve is more beautiful than any figure in classical mythology:

> Eve
> Undeckt, save with herself more lovely fair
> Then Wood-Nymph, or the fairest Goddess feign'd
> Of three that in Mount Ida naked strove . . .
>
> (V, 379–82)

The nuptial bower is likewise superior:

> In shadie Bower
> More sacred and sequesterd, though but feignd,
> Pan or Silvanus never slept, nor Nymph,
> Nor Faunus haunted . . .
>
> (IV, 705–8)

At the most the ancient fable may figure an excellence which is realized only in the Christian account. In the description of the Garden:

Thus was this place,
A happy rural seat of various view;
Groves whose rich Trees wept odorous Gumms and Balme,
Others whose fruit burnisht with Golden Rinde
Hung amiable, Hesperian Fables true,
If true, here only, and of delicious taste . . .

(IV, 246–51)

Of course we don't assume that others, who are not serious Christian poets, credit the truth of myth merely because they don't make a point of its falsehood. Classical allusion is too often just a manner of speaking in a literate way, gracefully, or a source of metaphor in which the factual truth is irrelevant. We take it as a matter of course for what it contributes. It is no problem for a poet—such as Jonson or Herrick or Milton in his earlier poetry—who is writing a poem in which he can be completely at home in the literary tradition, that is, one who has accepted the assumptions, the given, in the art as it has come down to him. This poet may be personally a complete Christian, but when he speaks as a poet in the recognized literary tradition, other allowances and requirements are on him, just as differing requirements are on him when he turns from his poetry. Ordinarily, then, it is not necessary to go so much out of the way to avoid the appearance of crediting these falsehoods. Milton, however, faces both requirements at once, for he intends to speak in the literary idiom on the most serious Christian subject.

II

Apart from the evidence reviewed above there is in *Paradise Lost* a more fundamental strain, or tension, that is properly and usefully regarded from the perspective used so far. This strain has been variously recognized but, in general, we can say that it originates in a conflict between the literary and the religious requirements Milton faced in the kind of poem he proposed. Milton's, or anyone's, difficulties in presenting the Christian scheme of things in a 'classical' epic are fairly obvious. The supernatural Christian material, we have often heard, is full of inconveniences for the epic narrative. Recognition of this difficulty is as old as Milton criticism, and it is common to admirers as well as detractors. Walter Raleigh, in the work that has served as a point of departure for much modern comment, calls the subject 'wildly intractable'[4] and observes that 'Milton himself . . .was well aware that his subject demanded something of the nature of a *tour de force*. He had to give physical, geometric embodiment to a far-reaching scheme of abstract speculation and thought,—part of it very reluctant to such a treatment.'[5] Basil Willey, who describes the Christian fable as 'bristling with inconveniences', explains some of the difficulty and indicates its source:

> Owing to its historical development in union with Greek philosophy, Christianity was in the peculiar position of possessing not only a Hellenic God who was the Absolute of theology, but also a Hebrew Jehovah whose personality and behaviour were not altogether unlike those of 'the gods'. The discrepancy between the two conceptions would be felt to be due to the progressive quality of the divine revelation, whereby one kind of relationship between God and man would be fitting before Christ's appearance, and another afterwards. In the seventeenth century, however Hebraically many Puritans thought and spoke about God, there is no doubt that for the best minds (Milton of course among them) God was 'omnipotent immutable, immortal, infinite', and this meant difficulty for any one who should speak of divine subjects in poetry, which can only proceed by giving to everything it touches 'a local habitation and a name'.[6]

Willey goes on to point out that the consciousness of this problem appears also in Boileau's pronouncement that the Christian faith is unsuitable for poetic treatment,[7] and in Johnson's censure of *Lycidas* for its mingling of 'trifling fictions' and 'the most sacred and awful truths'.[8] There is even some of this feeling, it seems to me, in the apprehensive tone at the beginning of Marvell's poem of praise prefacing the 1674 edition of *Paradise Lost*:

the Argument
Held me a while misdoubting his Intent,
That he would ruine (for I saw him strong)
The sacred Truths to Fable and old Song.[9]

The same consciousness of the fundamental difficulty lies behind Johnson's criticism of Milton's confused treatment of 'immateriality',[10] a consciousness that is shared by Macaulay in his defence of Milton against Johnson's strictures.[11] A defender of Milton in our day, Douglas Bush, shows a similar awareness of the problem when he speaks of 'the gulf between Milton's material and his theme'.[12] Critics apparently agree, then, that the difficulty exists in *Paradise Lost*, though they may differ on the question of whether Milton surmounts it or not.

Familiar as these observations are, it may be worthwhile, nevertheless, to consider just how we are aware of this conflict between literary and religious requirements as we read the poem, observing what lies behind the commonly accepted generalizations concerning the 'intractability' of Milton's subject in the epic form. It is proper to ask, at what places in the poem are we particularly conscious of a stress between these conflicting demands on Milton? I propose first, therefore, a modest review of the poem as through the eyes of an ordinary Christian reader, setting forth the issue where it would seem to be most crucial for the success of the poem, i.e. in its affective consequences.

The description of Mammon in Book 1 is a good example of the general kind of thing we are concerned with:

> Mammon led them on,
> Mammon, the least erected Spirit that fell
> From heav'n, for ev'n in heav'n his looks and thoughts
> Were always downward bent, admiring more
> The riches of Heav'ns pavement, trod'n Gold,
> Then aught divine or holy else enjoy'd
> In vision beatific . . .
>
> (678–84)

The passage is successful, I take it, as a realistic and dramatically appropriate characterization. For Mammon to take his part in the narrative it is required that he be represented with recognizable human traits and motives, that the characterization explain and justify his behaviour in the literal action the poem gives us. This is not an impossible requirement, but it has its risks. We realize the risks when we look beyond the admittedly successful local effect of the passage and think of what it implies about Heaven. Unless we forget a great deal of our Christian belief, we are immediately troubled. How can Mammon as an unfallen spirit show these signs of avarice? Can we picture him as one of the blessed admiring the streets of gold for their wealth? The image is absurd. Isn't this a sin before Sin had entered the universe—as Milton tells us elsewhere? (II, 746–61.) What, furthermore, can gold or wealth mean to unfallen Mammon in such a situation? Can we avoid the simple objection that gold buys things and *that* is its significance on Earth, but in Heaven, before the existence of sin or the Earth, it can have no such significance? Furthermore, if we believe that God is perfection and Heaven is perfect bliss then it is a terrible reduction of heavenly existence to picture one so high in spiritual excellence bent over musing on the worth of Heaven's pavement. These objections apply to this passage in addition to any continuing discomfort we may feel over Milton's grossly pictorial presentation of the furniture of Heaven, the streets of gold, etc., that is before us throughout the poem.

The passage is apparently appropriate in one way, yet we cannot abide it in another. It is appropriate to an interest in the realistic action of the narrative, and to have understandable action we ordinarily must have psychologically believable characters, i.e. characters understood to some extent in human terms. This is an obvious risk, however, when the character also has a significance in an ideal realm in which some traits are out of place. The Christian heaven, not to go into its historical development under the influence of otherworldly philosophies, has become such an ideal realm, unlike other possible heavens poets may deal with—certainly unlike the 'heaven' of the classical poets. Whether it is convenient for his poem or not, Milton just can't talk about the Christian heaven without the traditional conceptions creeping in; these associations go with the very words he uses. Here the picture of Mammon implies characteristics of Heaven that clash with our traditional conceptions of it. This is not just a religious complaint nor is it just a matter of logic; it is an artistic complaint too, for we are recognizing that the poet may not, for his immediate purposes, be able to disengage these disrupting spiritual conceptions from his material. The weight of association may be too much for him, out of his control, stronger than the meanings he would shape in the immediate context of his poem.[13] Certainly the freight of meaning attached to Christian references would make the use of Christian cosmography potentially a very ticklish business anyway considering that the professed models for so much else in the poem, the classical epics, have such a different cosmography—so philosophically unladen, anthropomorphic, and primitive. In recognizing this, of course, we only repeat the misgivings of many critic's of Milton's own time and later, but the fact is as important for our present purpose as it is obvious, and it is well to see it clearly.

To complain as we do above is not just to refer the danger to matters outside the poem, though we may feel strongly that the poet cannot ignore the inherited significance of his material. It is also, for this poem, a danger within the poem, for the traditional theological scheme is the official subject of the poem and these passages will be further out of place if they conflict with the public doctrine the poem outwardly supports elsewhere. Merely by writing a realistic narrative poem on such a subject, then, Milton is making himself vulnerable to an undeniably fundamental Christian perspective. He is not only in danger of making a gross reduction of his subject, but of making, mainly by implication, incongruous and inconsistent statements about it, statements that may provoke from the reader conflicting and contradictory responses from one passage to another. Milton is everywhere skirting these dangers but in some places the ice is thinner than in others. It may seem perverse to raise much sand over something that appears so much a part of the 'given' of the poem, the 'way' of the epic assumed from the start, but let us adopt for a while the perspective that resists Milton's reduction of traditional religious conceptions to this sphere and, at least, see what can be said.

It is not surprising that we feel the tug against Christian belief most strongly in places where overt parallels to classical models are most obvious. Certainly our forgetfulness of the Christian scheme is most necessary for Milton when his heaven appears most like Olympus, when

> from dance to sweet repast they turn
> Desirous; all in Circles as they stood,
> Tables are set, and on a sudden pil'd
> With Angels Food, and rubied Nectar flows
> In Pearl, in Diamond, and massie Gold,
> Fruit of delicious Vines, the growth of Heav'n.
> (V, 630–5)

when

> exercis'd Heroic Games
> Th' unarmed Youth of Heav'n, but nigh at hand
> Celestial Armourie, Shields, Helmes, and Speares,
> Hung high with Diamond flaming, and with Gold.
> (IV, 551–4)

This is an old complaint, but the echo of epic models extends, of course, beyond these outright similarities of event, the games, feasts, scales in the sky, etc., and the tension is not limited to these crude resemblances to the earlier epics. Consider the whole martial atmosphere in the poem, an atmosphere that is apparently necessary to the kind of poem Milton conceives from his epic models, whatever his Christian fable supplies. Milton, certainly, is concerned to emphasize the martial atmosphere even where his Christian fable does not require it. Not only are we always conscious that his characters are heroic warriors, but we are presented with warlike machinery and technical military terms at every opportunity. The setting of the watch on the Garden, which is presented with a fine technical and professional savour, is typical:

> And from thir Ivorie Port the Cherubim
> Forth issuing at th' accustomed hour stood armed
> To thir night watches in warlike Parade,
> When Gabriel to his next in power thus spake.

Uzziel, half these draw off, and coast the South
With strictest watch; these other wheel the North,
Our circuit meets full West. As flame they part
Half wheeling to the Shield, half to the Spear.

(IV, 778–85)

The heavenly company appears in martial array even before
Satan's revolt. At the great assembly

Innumerable before th' Almighties Throne
Forthwith from all the ends of Heav'n appeerd
Under thir Hierarchs in orders bright
Ten thousand thousand Ensignes high advanc'd,
Standards, and Gonfalons twixt Van and Reare
Streame in the Aire, and for distinction serve
Of Hierarchies, of Orders, and Degrees;
Or in thir glittering Tissues bear imblaz'd
Holy Memorials, acts of Zeale and Love
Recorded eminent.

(V, 585–94)

From our assumed point of view the disturbing question (that, for
the success of Milton's effect, should not arise) is a simple one:
Why this military appearance, this ranked army in Heaven, before
any discord was there? Will it not occur to the reader that arms
are for war? Is not what this implies about heavenly existence
hard to reconcile with our usual versions of that existence? At how
many points is the martial business, the epic business, at odds with
central Christian conceptions? We learn that

the Towrs of Heav'n are filled
With Armed watch, that render all access
Impregnable; oft on the bordering Deep
Encamp thir Legions, or with obscure wing
Scout farr and wide into the Realm of night,
Scorning surprize.   .

(II, 129–34)

It is counter to logic that Omniscience could be surprised. The

Christian God cannot be surprised. To suggest that he *can* be not only violates the logic demanded by theology but it goes against the instincts given us in the usual Christian training. But Milton here, for purposes of immediate local effect, suspends the characteristics of the Christian God in favour of a personage that, it is hinted, may be surprised. This is necessary to give an illusion of significance to the action of the martial characters, mainly the angels. In a situation such as this Milton must allow suggestions which, if pursued, are contradictory to his own and the orthodox conception of God.

The incongruity of the martial bustle is, indeed, nowhere more apparent than in the picture of God the Father. It is an unstable portrait, likely to be shattered for us by the slightest thought of the God commonly apprehended by Christians. To repeat some truisms, the God that Milton had to put into a narrative poem presented him with a problem appallingly without precedent in his models. This God differs from other possible epic deities or heroes in that He is so much a being apprehended by the reason, beyond the senses, the personification of philosophically conceived attributes—omniscience, omnipotence, omnipresence, perfection, completeness, self-sufficiency, independence. How can such a being be drawn into the busy action of the epic? We grant that this is the God of the philosopher and the theologian, and that the popular imagination has often provided other images of God that poets can work with more easily, yet this philosophically awesome God is the God we must recognize as the Christian God in the end. And certainly He, the God that has come down to us from Aristotle and Thomas, is a figure naturally forced into our minds in any poem that proposes to expound directly the Christian scheme of things at the most exalted levels.

In making God a character in this kind of poem, then, Milton must satisfy two very dissimilar requirements. On the one hand is the requirement of the epic:[14] grand action, martial bustle, motivated and realistic behaviour in human terms. We may, if we wish, call this a requirement in the classical literary tradition. On the other hand is the unavoidable conception in any treatment of God in the Christian tradition: the mystically exalted image given us by our theology and worshipped in our churches. Milton must do justice to this image of God merely because it is there, inseparable from the Christian tradition, bound into its vocabulary. Needless to say, these requirements pull against each other. The tension between them neatly represents, in little, the whole literary-religious tension we are concerned with throughout the poem. It may be noted, too, in passing, that this tension might just as suitably be called a classical-Christian tension inasmuch as it very neatly represents the clash between those two traditions in their essential features.

In the immediate problem, we see that the result of these incompatible demands is that God is cast in two roles, one proper to the martial bustle of the epic, the other proper to the metaphysical deity of Christian theology. The role Milton would have uppermost varies with the immediate interest at each place in the poem. In His theological role God says, 'I am who fill infinitude' (VII, 165f.). In this role He is often described directly, the acknowledged God of the poem. The angels hail Him:

> Thee Father first they sung Omnipotent,
> Immutable, Immortal, Infinite,
> Eternal King; thee Author of all being,
> Fountain of Light, thy self invisible
> Amidst the glorious brightness where thou sit'st
> Thron'd inaccessible . . .
>
> (III, 372–7)

But in a situation such as that following Satan's defection, Milton's God must be cast in the role of commander-in-chief of an anthropomorphic band of warriors, a monarch battling rebellion. In this role, however, the figure conflicts with that of the Christian God, which is always unavoidably in the background, and the first role strains against the second:

> Son, thou in whom my glory I behold
> In full resplendence, Heir of all my might,
> Neerly it now concernes us to be sure
> Of our Omnipotence, and with what Arms

> We mean to hold what anciently we claim
> Of Deity or Empire, such a foe
> Is rising, who intends to erect his Throne
> Equal to ours, throughout the spacious North;
> Nor so content, hath in his thought to try
> In battel, what our Power is, or our right.
> Let us advise, and to this hazard draw
> With speed what force is left, and all imploy
> In our defence, lest unawares we lose
> This our high place, our Sanctuarie, our Hill.
>
> (V, 719–32)

For our interest in the literal action of the poem, Milton properly plays for some suspense in the coming battle, but the passage is full of terms we cannot credit at full value. How can Omnipotence be concerned to be sure of His omnipotence? What have arms to do with holding His empire? When God says

> Let us advise, and to this hazard draw
> With speed what force is left, and all imploy
> In our defence

He is speaking the language of a beleaguered monarch in Shakespeare's history plays. 'Hazard' suggests chance, but there can be no chance. The final suggestion, 'lest unawares we lose this our high place', is a suggestion inconceivable in its implications. How can Omniscience be caught unawares, surprised?

When God speaks in the epic role He actually relinquishes His metaphysical attributes. He relinquishes His omnipotence, for example, in His comments on Satan after Satan has broken the bonds God set:

> Onely begotten Son, seest thou what rage
> Transports our adversarie, whom no bounds
> Prescrib'd, no barrs of Hell, nor all the chains
> Heapt on him there, nor yet the main Abyss
> Wide interrupt can hold . . .
>
> (III, 80–4)

The fact is that any bond an omnipotent God sets *can* hold him. And the bars and chains would have nothing to do with holding him. If we are impressed with the strength and size of Hell gate, then, we are impressed with an irrelevance. From the present point of view, *any* awe that we feel at the images of physical magnitude and power is, on reflection, unjustified and naive, for they are all irrelevant—and it hardly should astound us that Omnipotence can produce them.

We might go so far as to say that wherever Milton feeds our interest in the martial action, the fundamental 'epic' appeal of the poem, he is led to absurdities in the religious scheme, not necessarily in what he says directly but in what he implies. It is an advantage to him if we do not think very much about what he says, if we do not take him seriously. If we do take the meaning of his terms in their full sense, realizing the kind of existence they imply, we find that those terms inevitably subvert the 'official' scheme he gives us elsewhere. The effect that succeeds with us, then, is purely local, proper only to the immediate scene and our one interest in it, the literal surface action.

This includes most of the business performed by the angels, which is made impressive and significant at the expense of a diminished God. While we are enjoying the martial action we like to think that it is to some purpose, and Milton is at pains to supply purposes. Raphael, requesting Adam's story of the creation, gives a plausible kind of justification for his troops' activity:

> For I that Day was absent, as befell,
> Bound on a voyage uncouth and obscure,
> Farr on excursion toward the Gates of Hell;
> Squar'd in full Legion (such command we had)
> To see that none thence issu'd forth a spie,
> Or enemie, while God was in his work,
> Least hee incens't at such eruption bold,
> Destruction with Creation might have mixt.
>
> (VIII, 229–36)

The last two lines suggest that God may become confused, lose self-control, and in anger destroy accidentally the world he intends to create. This, if applied at all to the Christian God, is of course unthinkable. Why does Milton do this? Here it is clear that the idea makes sense of the physical action of his plot; it gives reason and motive to the martial activity of the angelic guard, which is always in danger of appearing completely superfluous.

In the heat of the moment, when they are acting most realistically like Homeric warriors, Milton's angels are most likely to disorganize our picture of God and heaven, saying things that they, and Milton, don't really mean. When Gabriel and Satan face each other outside the Garden, their 'horrid fray' incipient, exchanging the customary defiant speeches before battle, Gabriel says

> who more then thou
> Once fawn'd, and cring'd, and servilly ador'd
> Heav'ns awful Monarch?
>
> (IV, 958–60)

Though the scene has a 'human' interest in the fronting of two well-realized personalities, Gabriel denies in a few words the absolute adorability of God and puts Satan's unfallen service in an impossible light, giving us a sin before sin was possible.

The main source of our discomfort in these passages is that there is a difference, or disharmony, between the local, immediate effect of a passage and the overall scheme of the poem—or, at least, the official Christian scheme that the poem gives the impression of supporting. We call his effects 'local' because they can only be realized in the immediate context: if we pursue the meanings into the larger context of the whole poem we are led into confusion and contradiction. Milton's Christian vocabulary apparently arouses expectations and suggestions that cannot be managed in his epic vocabulary. This all may seem like a fine elaboration of the obvious, and I would not multiply evidence unnecessarily, but, before relinquishing our 'hostile' perspective, I would like to analyse in detail some few passages that, it seems to me, focus the foregoing issues fairly well and permit a statement of the difficulty in its broadest terms.

The first two passages I shall present deserve attention not only because they represent clear cases of epic business doing violence to the Christian scheme, of the unassimilated local effect, but also because they profess to give what is often taken to justify the literal reduction of spiritual matters: a metaphorical meaning. Since this is a common and proper justification of literal details, it will be well to anticipate the later argument by noting this evidence along the way. First, the scene at Hell Gate. Satan approaches Sin and Death and calls out to Death:

> Whence and what art thou, execrable shape,
> That dar'st, though grim and terrible, advance
> Thy miscreated Front athwart my way
> To yonder Gates?
>
> (II, 681–4)

Death answers with similar vituperation:

> Back to thy punishment,
> False fugitive, and to thy speed add wings,
> Least with a whip of Scorpions I pursue
> Thy lingring, or with one stroke of this Dart
> Strange horror seise thee, and pangs unfelt before.
>
> (II, 699–703)

Here are the epic warriors' defiant speeches before combat, the exchange of taunts and threats. It is a typical piece of martial business. As epic warriors these personages must threaten each other and make ready for exciting single combat. But, besides being warriors, they stand for conceptions in the theological scheme. Death personifies an element in that scheme and Satan has a symbolic part, too, as the Author of Evil. In these roles what can they threaten each other with? The Author of Evil sired Death; what would be the meaning of wounding him now? Even less conceivable, at the allegorical level, is Death's threat to strike Satan with the fatal dart, i.e. kill him. Death kill Evil? What could this mean? Clearly Milton would like to suspend for the moment the symbolic import he has given his characters. Yet he cannot do this completely for nothing can actually *happen*, nothing that he cannot forget later when he wants to take advantage of their symbolic significance for 'religious' purposes. We are left with one of the many shows of combat full, up to a point, with all the epic machinery, but drained of further significance. There can be no real fight.

The interposition of Sin between the combatants illustrates even better the division between the realistically motivated local effect in which the characters are simple Homeric battlers and the theological scheme within which they must function as symbols. Sin makes the psychologically and dramatically appropriate cry against the fight between son and father:

> O Father, what intends thy hand, she cry'd
> Against thy only Son? What fury O Son,
> Possesses thee to bend that mortal Dart
> Against thy Fathers head?
>
> (II, 727–30)

The appeal to filial and paternal feelings, family sentiments, however convenient in the immediate context, is out of place when applied to the Author of Evil, Sin, and Death. What should Death care for his father's reverend head?

We may ask whether this is not putting too fine a point on the symbolic significance of these characters. Yet, it is not we who force their symbolic role but Milton. Indeed, immediately after the above scene he gives a history of Sin and Death in which their symbolic significance is paramount and quite appropriate to the theological scheme. Sin springs from Satan's brain when he first plots rebellion; Death, in turn, is conceived in Sin by Satan. Milton wants it both ways. Rather than satisfying two requirements in one, the proper operation of symbol (I take it), Milton satisfies them alternately. This resembles his procedure throughout the poem, where alternation seems to be the principle by which he arranges his effects, rather than mutual support. The full realization of one effect is a handicap to the full realization of another, for the successive effects do not reinforce and extend each other; they contradict and undermine each other.

The personification of Chaos and eldest Night exhibits the same difficulty:

> when strait behold the Throne
> Of Chaos, and his dark Pavilion spread
> Wide on the wasteful Deep; with him Enthron'd
> Sat Sable-vested Night, eldest of things,
> The Consort of his Reign; and by them stood
> Orcus and Ades, and the dreaded name
> Of Demogorgon; Rumor next and Chance,
> And Tumult and Confusion all imbroild,
> And Discord with a thousand various mouths.
>
> (II, 959–67)

The impression left by the conversation that follows is that this realm is not a party to the conflict, that it is a 'non-belligerent' third country co-existing with Heaven even before the rebellion. It might even be gathered here that this monarchy is older than Heaven, or God, if Night is really 'eldest of things' (though Milton's term 'things' may leave it open whether God is included here). The third country serves the need for 'various action' that must fill the epic. Making Chaos and his train into the courtly personages of a military power furthers the realistic activity in the poem. They are needed as people for this activity, the martial bustle, and appear before us with a throne, a court, and affairs of state. But they also represent abstractions in a cosmography that has its own requirements, and if we attempt to press their allegorical significance further than the local scene, we once again run into difficulty. God puts forth his virtue into chaos to create beings, we are told elsewhere (XII 168–73), but here is Chaos set up even before the revolt with full regal machinery in a realm separate from God, possibly as old as God, and implicitly hostile to God. He naturally sides with Satan. What can we make of God's omnipotence and omnipresence in such a situation, or of the symbolic role of Satan as the great antagonist, the originator of evil? We obviously end in confusion. Here, therefore, we must say that one requirement is met at the expense of the other. Milton's real skill in the passage, it appears, must lie in his ability to slur over these symbolic significances and keep our view focused on the surface action.

Some temptingly handy terms for describing the whole difficulty are put, almost inadvertently it seems, into the mouth of Gabriel himself. As 'Chief of the Angelic Guards' at the Gate of Paradise, Gabriel, after being warned of Satan's proximity, replies to Uriel that

> in at this Gate none pass
> The vigilance here plac't, but such as come
> Well known from Heav'n; and since Meridian hour
> No creature thence: if Spirit of other sort,
> So minded, have overleapt these earthie bounds
> On purpose, hard thou knowst it to exclude
> Spiritual substance with corporeal barr.
>
> (IV, 579–85)

Here is Gabriel with the 'Celestial Armourie, Shields, Helmes, and Speares' nigh at hand, his legions close by exercising at 'Heroic Games'. It is the characteristic representation of the warrior angels, the business that makes up so much of the action of the poem. But the last line cuts the props from under all of it, not just here but in the whole poem. Gabriel says that to exclude the spiritual with the corporeal is 'hard', speaking in the manner of a lieutenant faced with a difficult assignment. It is indeed hard; it is impossible. All the corporeal bars are useless, all the corporeal swords, shields, spears, and martial machinery. To think to prevent Satan, a spirit, from entering Paradise with all this paraphernalia of the Angelic Guards is absurd. All the corporeal trappings are irrelevant, here and in the whole martial bustle that captures our interest and concern elsewhere. The apparatus of one sphere, the material, the panoply likened to earth's gear, has nothing to do with the other sphere, the spiritual. It would be a denial of a fundamental Christian belief for it to be so, for the corporeal world to have power over the spiritual. The assignment is 'hard' for Gabriel partly because to succeed would be to mock the dualism so often insisted on in Christian belief, the distinction between spirit and matter.

It is a feeling for the necessity of this distinction that, I take it, lies behind Samuel Johnson's complaint against the 'confusion of spirit and matter' in the war in Heaven.[15] Though the confusion is naturally at its height there, where the epic demands are most exclusively satisfied, the observation may well be applied in a broader sense to the whole poem. For Gabriel to say, then, that it would be 'hard' for corporeal bars to stop Satan is to remind us how considerably the whole action of the poem as an epic, the action drawn from classical models, is of corporeal bars in one sense or another. Most of the things that are done appear as a manipulation of corporeal bars, the action of earth no matter how enhanced the scale may be. Nearly all the echoes of the epic, the events that satisfy the requirements of the genre, all of these are merely various stagings of the corporeal, behind which lies the assumption that corporeal bars can do something. But we know, and Milton knows, that in this realm they can't. Yet, we might have forgotten this if Gabriel, with his reference to 'spiritual substance', had not reminded us of it.

After such a reminder, we complain, not so much against the corporeal in itself, but against Milton's getting us so interested and concerned in it—something so unmeaning and irrelevant. Certainly the actual significance of the martial scenes seems out of all proportion to the rhetorical emphasis Milton gives them, playing the scenes always for suspense, horror, awe, portentousness. We have Satan and Gabriel facing each other outside the Garden, exchanging defiant speeches, as they prepare to fight:

> While thus he [Satan] spake, th' Angelic Squadron bright
> Turnd fierie red, sharpning in mooned hornes
> Thir Phalanx, and began to hemm him round
> With ported Spears . . .
> On th' other side Satan allarm'd
> Collecting all his might dilated stood,
> Like Teneriff or Atlas unremov'd:
> His stature reacht the Skie, and on his Crest
> Sat horror Plum'd; nor wanted in his graspe
> What seemd both Spear and Shield; now dreadful deeds
> Might have ensu'd, nor onely Paradise

In this commotion, but the Starrie Cope
Of Heav'n perhaps, or all the Elements
At least had gon to rack, disturbed and torne
With violence of this conflict, had not soon
Th' Eternal to prevent such horrid fray
Hung forth in Heav'n his golden Scales . . .

(IV, 977–97)

The sight of the scales prevents the fight, and Gabriel says

Satan, I know thy strength, and thou knowst mine,
Neither our own but giv'n; what follie then
To boast what Arms can doe, since thine no more
Then Heav'n permits, nor mine, though doubl'd now
To trample thee as mire . . .

(IV, 1006–10)

There has been an impressive rattling of swords but this is another
one of the fights that never come off. Milton has, in fact, obtained
all the effects of epic military action except for the actual combat.
The suggestion of 'dreadful deeds' ensuing gives only the flavour
of seriousness to the show of arms, a seeming justification of the
martial pomp for the immediate awe of the reader. The deeds will
be as dreadful as God allows, and Milton's suggestion that the
combat was not permitted in order to prevent the destruction of
Earth is not legitimate. Satan could be made as impotent here as
he is later when God transforms him into a serpent. The whole
scene, like the apparition of the scales, is staged for purposes
demanded by the imitation of classical epic. There can be no
contest, for the antagonists fight only as a show, with the power
given them. 'What follie then to boast what Arms can doe,'
says Gabriel, reminding us, almost inadvertently, of the larger
perspective on the whole scene—and on all such scenes. The implications of the question make us pause. What folly to boast what
arms can do? What folly then for us to get interested in the scene,
to be awed by 'horror Plum'd' and the phalanx of spears. What
folly for Milton to linger impressively on the military dazzle
when the same two angels face each other in the war in heaven:

for likest Gods they seemd,
Stood they or mov'd, in stature, motion, arms
Fit to decide the Empire of great Heav'n.
Now wav'd thir fierie Swords, and in the Aire
Made horrid Circles; two broad Suns thir Shields
Blaz'd opposite, while expectation stood
In Horror . . .

(VI, 301-7)

Gabriel's unwitting insight applies to the poem's whole concern
with what arms can do, the continued pre-occupation with corporeal bars. It is an insight that undercuts the whole surface
panoply of epic action. This is seen to be separate from and
meaningless for the decision of spiritual matters. It appeals to us
on other grounds. Yet, and here is an index of Milton's skill, the
reader is most of the time given the feeling that great things are
being decided by this bustle. Milton works continually to keep up
interest in the action of his poem, and impending fights must look
important. There will never be a real contest, but Milton would
like to give the *feel* of a real contest. His problem, most pronounced
in the war in heaven, is to make a contest of the incontestable as,
in handling the angels generally, he must make armour for the
impregnable, wounds for the fleshless, weapons for the invincible,
and jobs for the jobless. Into such tasks his double requirement
forces him.

We have called these corporeal reductions 'offences' against the
theological scheme. It is not necessary to detail how they transgress
against this or that point in orthodox theology, and it is no part of
my purpose to list particular heresies. What we are concerned with
here is a fundamental difference in spirit or attitude between the
world Milton actually evokes and the spiritual world of Christianity, the world that has his official allegiance. In the world his
narrative implies, there is, in Johnson's phrase, a confusion of spirit
and matter. This confusion in effect eliminates 'spirit' as we
normally conceive it and, philosophically speaking, denies Christian dualism, though Milton continues to use the accustomed language of dualism and gives the appearance of satisfying our expectations with respect to it. Insofar as this dualism, the emphatic

distinction between spirit and matter, soul and sense, is at the core of Christian belief, Milton 'offends' against the Christian scheme of things. This heresy in his fundamental approach to his material is, it seems to me, more serious than any of the particular departures from specific points of doctrine. Indeed, his specific departures may be seen as consequences of this fundamental departure. This is uncomfortable enough as a religious problem but it becomes very awkward as an artistic problem too since Milton cannot rest in monism but must try to have what he wants in both spheres. This continual shifting of the ground, the absence of a firm metaphysical foundation, may well account for most of the inconsistencies we have just reviewed.

In trying to spell out some of the reading difficulties that have long been admitted, we can, at least, recognize the strength of the tension between the requirements Milton tries to satisfy. Up to this point we must say that the tension is destructive. If the passages just reviewed have been read fairly and seriously, then the poem is not only at cross purposes with the Christian scheme it claims to propound, but it is at cross purposes with itself. Milton's attempt to satisfy two incompatible requirements seems, beyond local and temporary effects, to satisfy neither. We come to this belief by believing seriously what Milton says at each place, i.e. by trying to be good readers, by keeping the whole poem in mind as we read. It is just this that works our defeat, for the split in the poem is obscured only by our forgetfulness, our lack of real interest and serious concern. We must have a child's delight in the gorgeous martial bustle and a theologian's satisfaction in the official religious scheme, but we must keep our two reactions separate. Our responses can never be simultaneous, can never reinforce each other. For by bringing in our knowledge of the theological scheme we make the 'awesome' epic action look foolish; by succumbing to the impressive epic action that Milton treats with such rhetorical emphasis we make the theological scheme look absurd. We feel that in *Paradise Lost* there is not only an improper reduction and transformation of Milton's inherited material, but a confusion of purpose even in his reduced version of that material. The result is incongruity, inconsistency and confusion.

III

We may now try to test the validity of this reading in the face of possible objections. First, it will be noticed that the criticisms above are not the same as those complaints against Milton that have been so well answered recently. They are not part of the general opposition to Milton classified by Charles Williams into four kinds of complaint: '(i) that Milton was a bad man; (ii) that Milton was, especially, a proud man . . . (iii) that Milton's verse is hard, sonorous, and insensitive; (iv) that Milton's subject was remote and uninteresting.'[16] The complaints against Milton the man are irrelevant here, nothing has been said about the verse, and Milton's subjects, both official and unofficial, are potentially very interesting. The complaints can be made by a good Christian who understands the epic and appreciates ritual; i.e. they need not be made by the peculiarly modern reader C. S. Lewis excoriates in his *Preface to Paradise Lost*.[17]

It should also be recognized that, though the present perspective is 'hostile' and resistant, it is not arbitrary or artificial. It is, I believe, a normal enough Christian perspective. Milton evokes this perspective himself by his use of the traditional Christian vocabulary. No attempt has been made to justify such a perspective by this or that written creed, or by a majority sect; this is not really relevant, just as attempts to justify Milton by showing that this or that heterodoxy of his was actually held somewhere in the seventeenth century are not relevant. It is a matter of attitude or spirit, a way of looking at the world, and in this we may be closer to the normal seventeenth-century reader than some of his heterodox contemporaries. If the word 'normal' seems to beg the question, then we can only appeal to the 'normal' meanings of the words Milton uses, for they take their meaning from the primary tradition. 'Spirit' means spirit, 'omniscience' means omniscience, and so on. We know this by being 'normal' readers in the Christian tradition; we resist attempts to make them mean something else. We may further claim the right to be Milton's readers in this way on the basis of his own claim to make his poem 'doctrinal to a nation'. Certainly Milton appeals to our orthodox attitudes often enough in the poem itself when it is to his purpose.

Before trying to find arguments that might answer our initial reading, it is necessary to eliminate those that clearly cannot. There are, at the beginning, three common defences of Milton's procedure that we cannot allow ourselves. Yet they must be discussed since, if admitted, they would vitiate the objections that have been raised. The first refuses to admit that any problem exists, the second excuses the defects by referring them to the demands of the genre, and the third excuses them by ascribing them to inconveniences in the Christian faith itself.

For the reader who defends Milton by refusing to admit any problem there is no difference between the world Milton evokes and the heaven Milton, he, and other Christians believe in. He accepts literally the furniture of heaven as given. There is no difference in kind between matter and spirit, natural and supernatural. Heaven is merely built on a more exalted material scale— and properly so. This reader accepts Milton as a monist; he is one too. Certainly a great variety of conceptions have taken the name Christian, particularly in the popular imagination, and all we can say of this view is, 'Wear it in health.' The conceptions exist and they are called Christian. If we make this a principle, however, that permits them as a basis for a work that professes to 'justify the ways of God to men' we may have some legitimate reservations. Otherwise, by admitting the same principle consistently, we may find ourselves hard pressed to deny claims that *Green Pastures* may be doctrinal to a nation. These reservations apply even before we object to the internal illogicalities in *Paradise Lost*, where even the literal scheme is not consistent.

At bottom this is the view held by C. S. Lewis. It enables him to dismiss Johnson's criticism plausibly:

Johnson finds a 'confusion of spirit and matter' pervading Milton's whole account of the war in Heaven. But Johnson approached it under a misconception; according to him Milton 'saw that immateriality supplied no images' and therefore 'invested' his angels with 'form and matter'—in other words Johnson believed that the corporeality of Milton's angels was a *poetic fiction.* He expected to see the poet's real belief peeping through the fiction and thought he saw what he expected. I once thought—perhaps most readers thought—the same. A new period in my appreciation of *Paradise Lost* began when I first found reason to believe that Milton's picture of the angels, though doubtless poetical in detail, is meant in principle as a literally true picture of what they probably were according to the up-to-date pneumatology of his century.[18]

Lewis then quotes the up-to-date pneumatologists to show that they believed in the corporeality of angels, as opposed to scholastic and modern belief. This pneumatology 'rules undisputed' throughout the poem. 'When once this has been grasped', says Lewis, 'most of the inconsistencies which Johnson thought he had discovered simply vanish.' Milton cannot confuse matter and spirit because he never shifts into the spiritual realm. In arguing this Lewis reveals himself as a determined monist and materialist. 'When Satan animates the toad', he says, 'this does not prove that he is immaterial, but only that his subtle body can penetrate a grosser body and contract itself to very small dimensions.' He does not understand that the matter-spirit distinction is a distinction in kind. Spirit, he believes, is only very, very rarefied matter. Surely this is an equivocation. Johnson properly understands that immateriality means *immateriality*, and not some special material with a new name. No matter how small Satan makes himself, down to the last molecule, he can never animate the toad in this material way. The turn of mind Lewis exhibits is of the kind that would get infinity by adding zeros to a number. Milton clearly does use a dualistic point of view when it is convenient, though elsewhere he may have it otherwise. The strain between the two points of view is still there, in the poem, not to be dismissed because at one place Milton presents a monistic cosmology, or because monism is possible to us—even if we were at complete liberty in the Christian scheme to have it so. The inconsistency with the Christian norm can never vanish, and the inconsistencies within the poem will not vanish, for Milton forces them on us. We make them vanish only by wearing blinders.

Furthermore, to justify Milton's procedure by the up-to-date pneumatology of his time is merely to shift the burden of responsibility, not eliminate it. To say that Milton intended it this way is no help either. So much the worse for the pneumatologists and his own intention. The proper question is whether he should have intended it this way (if we are to make sense of his other intentions) and whether characteristics of his angels are proper to his poem, regardless of where he found those characteristics.

Finally, what can Lewis mean by saying that the true, literal picture is 'doubtless poetical in detail'? Where does the truth stop and the poetical detail begin? We should know this if we are to be affected by the truth and not distracted by the detail. Suppose it is the 'poetical detail' that Milton seems most to employ in the effects he works for? How would we apply the distinction in the following description of Satan as a typical angel?

> And now a stripling Cherube he appeers,
> Not of the prime, yet such as in his face
> Youth smil'd Celestial, and to every Limb
> Sutable grace diffus'd, so well he feign'd;
> Under a Coronet his flowing haire
> In curles on either cheek plaid, wings he wore
> Of many a coloured plume sprinkl'd with Gold,
> His habit fit for speed succinct, and held
> Before his decent steps a Silver wand.
>
> (III, 636–44)

If we think of a department-store Christmas-window angel, have we been distracted by the poetical part or must we take these gold-flecked plumes as the literal truth about heaven?

T. S. Eliot, in his later pronouncement on Milton, similarly arrives at a 'new appreciation' and dismisses Johnson's criticism by accepting Milton's world as given:

Most of the absurdities and inconsistencies to which Johnson calls attention, and which, so far as they can justly be isolated in this way, he properly condemns, will I think appear in a more correct proportion if we consider them in relation to this general judgment. I do not think that we should attempt to *see* very clearly any scene that Milton depicts: it should be accepted as a shifting phantasmagory. To complain, because we first find the arch-fiend 'chained on the burning lake', and in a minute or two see him making his way to shore, is to expect a kind of consistency which the world to which Milton has introduced us does not require.[19]

These are not real defences of *Paradise Lost* because they remove the difficulty, not by asking for a better, fully responsive reading of the poem, but by asking for a limited and reduced reading, a careless reading. They obscure the violence Milton does by asking us to do a violence to ourselves, making us strain to become different from the people we are when we read anything else. Lewis, in effect, asks us to become children, adopting a primitive, anthropomorphic faith. He gets his 'new appreciation' when he realizes that Milton intended his picture of Heaven to be a literally true one, and strains to adopt the view of a particular group of pneumatologists so that he can accept the picture. Eliot too, if I read him rightly, asks us to forget what we know, resting content with a 'shifting phantasmagory' where consistency is not required. But to call it a 'phantasmagory' is merely to give the problem a new name, as if phantasmagory were in itself always proper and permissible. Suppose we accept the term as a responsible description. A reader might say, 'Very well, logic is ended. But do not come around later clinching moral law, God's ways to men, and the ultimate foundations of the universe on the basis of your shifting phantasmagory. You have no answer if I prefer the "ghoul-haunted region of Weir".' For both Lewis and Eliot we are happiest with Milton's effects when we forget ourselves. We are to forget ourselves not just as Christians, but as serious readers of other parts of the poem.

The next path we must deny ourselves is the defence of Milton's procedure that takes the requirements of the genre as the proper measure of Milton's success. The argument, in brief, goes something like this: Before we can judge the work we must know *what* it is. Milton intended this poem to be an epic. An epic has certain characteristics, among them the very things that we object to. Once we understand the epic, get a taste for it, then the faults turn into beauties and we are satisfied. The martial equipage, heroic games, perilous journeys, marvellous buildings are all the traditional stuff of the epic. To complain against them is to criticize Milton for the very thing he intended.[20]

This is not a legitimate refuge for several reasons. First, we are faced with the question of how much the genre demands. Might not Milton have read the requirements of the epic genre poorly, thinking that he had to include things that are not necessary at all, only superficial and crude accoutrements of the models he desired to imitate? On the other hand, even if these things are proper to the genre, it is still possible that Milton has the wrong genre for his subject or the wrong subject for his genre. Therefore, even if we grant the above argument, these questions, the crucial ones, are still to be argued. We don't answer the question by shifting the burden of justification to the genre and letting it go at that.

The third escape is to lay the blame on the Christian faith itself. Here we claim that since there are irrationalities and mysteries in Christian belief, Milton merely inherits these difficulties and cannot be expected to display them in a reasonable and consistent way. We cannot expect him to solve the great Christian paradoxes any better than the great theologians before him. We recognize that there is no logical way to reconcile God's omnipotence and man's free will; why expect Milton to do it in a poem? Inconsistencies are inevitable. Add to this the difficulty in making characters of the supernatural beings the Christian scheme gives him and you do not wonder that Milton's epic treatment of this subject is awkward but that it is convincing at all. We should sympathize with his dilemma and not ask more than is possible. Considering the extremely difficult problem he sets himself, it is astounding that he succeeds as well as he does.

This view sets the choice of a subject and the manner of treating it beyond argument, beyond, in fact, the responsibility of the poet. It is as if Milton were *forced* to treat this theme, using this material, in this particular kind of poem. But these are artistic decisions under the control of the poet; the results of his choice issue in the poem for us to judge. Our judgment should not be influenced by the fact that the poet has set himself a very difficult problem. To read a poem in this way is a little like going to hear a man who has learned to play the violin with his feet. We can marvel at his dexterity under such handicaps and sympathize with his problems, but that has nothing to do with our pleasure in the music. The art must be loved for the music we hear and not for our sympathy with the artist's problems, for that is another matter. In this analogy I would demean not Milton but the argument his defenders wrongly use.

None of these arguments, it seems to me, requires us to make any qualification of our original dissatisfaction in trying to read *Paradise Lost* seriously. Even if the arguments were valid their general tendency lies aslant the main issue, for on the whole they would satisfy only the objection to sensuous reduction and not affect the primary complaint against confusion of purpose, the disharmony of effects.

One qualification, however, is necessary before we even begin to develop a more compelling answer. We must recognize that there is some distortion involved in the very manner in which the reader's plight was here displayed. It must be admitted that a destructive analysis of isolated passages does not allow for some of the effects gained in a consecutive reading of the poem. In the latter the poet may well make us more receptive to things we find very irksome when we pull them out into the cold light. In effect, we did not succumb to the spell of the poem, did not let Milton prepare our feelings for each passage. Certainly Milton has a technique that anticipates our discomfort and, if it does not solve the problem logically, it may help solve it emotionally. This is the technique of illusion.

The illusion is of two kinds, corresponding to the two main requirements Milton faces. If he adheres to his theological scheme he must give the illusion that the martial bustle, the epic business, has some purpose and importance. If he adheres to the literal action of his epic narrative he must give the illusion that no violence is done to the theological conceptions his characters are inevitably involved with. Illusion is necessary because an actual harmony is impossible. How well Milton succeeds! He keeps our attention so well focused on the surface action that we hardly notice the disorganizing implications; yet when he uses the traditional vocabulary of Christianity it is as if his epic atmosphere had no implications at all. He slurs over the uncomfortable symbolic significance of his allegorical figures, then uses them for an impressive allegorical meaning. He has really two Gods, yet gives us the impression that they are one and the same. Such illusion is not properly a justification, but it is a palliative and its local success should be recognized in assessing our reactions through the poem.

If, now, we grant that our original perspective is secure from the three common defences considered above, and that Milton's skill at maintaining illusion only soothes but does not satisfy a sensitive reading, there is still the possibility that our reading may be corrected from another direction: It may not have been sensitive *enough*. Perhaps we have not seen the 'figure in the carpet' (if the phrase may be applied to Milton) and are near-sightedly ignoring clues Milton gives us to an all-embracing frame in which to put the poem. A more comprehensive interpretation is always possible and we must be ready to admit correction from it.

Such a prospect leads us to consider one kind of answer that is frequently made to one of the objections offered at the beginning of this chapter. It says that if we find the literal details damaging, then we are just too literal-minded, and miss the real import of these details, which lies in their metaphorical, or allegorical, significance. That is, the literal picture is justified by its correspondence to a world behind it, or, if not that rigid, by a meaning it figures with respect to that world. This is, in principle, a promising argument and no doubt many wrong-headed readings result from blindness here.

First, let us consider the possibility of a simple correspondence. We might say that the corporeal world described in *Paradise Lost* is a 'likeness' of the spiritual world. Milton encourages this view at several places in the poem. Raphael, for example, might well be speaking of Milton's general problem and method when he contemplates the task of conveying the exploits of spirits to human sense:

> High matter thou injoinst me, O prime of men,
> Sad task and hard, for how shall I relate
> To human sense th' invisible exploits
> Of warring Spirits, how without remorse
> The ruin of so many glorious once
> And perfet while they stood; how last unfould
> The secrets of another world, perhaps
> Not lawful to reveal? yet for thy good
> This is dispenc't, and what surmounts the reach
> Of human sense, I shall delineate so,
> By lik'ning spiritual to corporal forms,
> As may express them best, though what if Earth
> Be but the shaddow of Heav'n, and things therein
> Each to other like, more then on earth is thought?
>
> (V, 563–76)

At the end of the narrative Raphael repeats that he is 'measuring things in Heav'n by things on Earth' (VI, 893).

This view is also encouraged by the additional suggestion that all is presented in a consciously and necessarily reductive language. Says Raphael,

> Immediate are the Acts of God, more swift
> Then time or motion, but to human ears
> Cannot without process of speech be told,
> So told as earthly notion can receave.
>
> (VII, 176–9)

The impression of a reductive language is fostered in several places in the poem. In Book I the rebel angels are not called by their real names but by the 'new Names' they had got among 'the sons of Eve'. When speaking of the retreating waters, Raphael says,

> as Armies at the call
> Of Trumpet (for of Armies thou hast heard)
> Troop to thir Standard . . .
>
> (VII, 295–7)

reminding us that his whole story is still a 'likening', a metaphorical use of terms familiar to Adam.

Can this be applied to Milton's method in the whole poem? If it can, how does it affect our first approach to the poem? The latter question has a clear answer: if the literal picture is a 'likening', then the spiritual world need not be debased by a corporeal reduction; the philosophical reader's imagination is free to keep its own picture of supernatural existence. The epic trappings need not offend him. But the first question, upon which this one depends, is not so easily answered. The trouble begins when we leave Raphael's statements and ask what this or that may be likened to. If Milton's corporeal forms are a likeness of spiritual forms, then how are we to explain those passages where Milton dwells so lovingly at the literal level, compelling our awe at things awesome only in a material way and not for any correspondence with a world of spirit? What is all the literally grand furniture of heaven a likeness of? What are we to do with the 'Opal Towrs and Battlements adorn'd of living Saphire', the 'Kingly Palace Gate with Frontispiece of Diamond and Gold imbellisht, thick with sparkling orient Gemmes', the angel's plumes 'sprinkl'd with Gold'? Who reads these passages of plain physical glamour with any metaphorical significance in mind? If Earth shadows Heaven, what can these passages convey about Heaven, what can the correspondence be? If Milton intends them to figure grandeur and excellence then it is a strange kind of excellence he attributes to the Christian Heaven, an epitomized dazzle of the senses. Even if we allow him this intention we must recognize a clash with an unavoidable Christian belief about heavenly excellence: that the grandeur of Heaven as a spiritual ideal lies in its difference, in kind, from the material grandeur of Earth. But, of course, we are not really to think of any metaphorical correspondence when we read these passages. Milton is not concerned that we should.

But if a simple correspondence cannot be maintained, perhaps the surface detail is justified in that it figures a meaning proper to the official subject of the poem. Attempts to find such a meaning in particular passages are not very rewarding, however. Even where a metaphorical meaning seems to be intended we still can't justify the overlay of just plain physical glamour. Where Milton most emphasizes an allegorical meaning, as in the encounters with

Sin and Death and with Chaos and old Night, the symbolic significance is completely mixed up, as we have seen. The images evoked at the literal level do not reinforce the symbolic meaning but are actively counter to that meaning.

The hazards of a metaphorical interpretation, locally applied, are illustrated by Arnold Stein's justification of the war in heaven as metaphor.[21] Johnson's criticism is justified, he believes, if we take the war literally, 'but suppose the material action of the war does not exist for its literal and independent meaning, but is instead part of a complex metaphor?'[22] Stein, if I read him correctly, believes that Milton does not really strive for grandeur in his description of the battle, and that the arms used by both sides are made ridiculous. I cannot make out what Stein takes to be the correspondences in the complex metaphor but the whole martial activity and equipage is apparently not to be taken seriously but to be understood as part of a 'comedy' staged by God to show the limitations of Satan's kind of behaviour. The difficulty of this view is that nothing prevents us from applying the same standards to the rest of the martial bustle elsewhere in the poem, including all the military exercise of the good angels doing God's errands. Why should we claim that there is no attempt at grandeur here in the heavenly battle where the epic business is merely most intense (and hardest to swallow), and not do the same elsewhere? But in the other passages Milton is clearly trying to make his martial array as impressive as he can.

A metaphorical interpretation is particularly attractive because it seems to be supported by Milton's own well-known theory that God reveals Himself by a language of accommodation; that is, He accommodates His meaning to the understandings and capabilities of the lesser beings requiring instruction, but is not Himself totally revealed in this reduction. The truth, therefore, may be revealed in fable or parable with, however, one difference from other fables: God, who is all-powerful, can cause His fables to be acted out. They are 'true' then, in the sense that the events actually happened, but not exhaustively true in the sense that they give a complete revelation.[23]

Since we have not been able to find a satisfactory meaning

'figured' in the objectionable passages of epic business, perhaps we can use the accommodation theory to develop some perspective that puts the whole epic approach in an acceptable light—we want to say that this is the *way* God chose to fable.

A case can, I think, be made for such a perspective. We begin directly with the greatest source of discomfort, the picture of God the Father. Milton's double requirement, we have seen, forces his God into two roles, one for his epic functions, another for his Christian or metaphysical functions. The characteristics of one role are incongruous in the other and the two roles clash. But suppose we establish a relation between the roles? A great difficulty, it has been said, is that the Christian God has no place in the bustle of the epic and cannot properly be treated by its necessarily reductive language. If, however, He is not a proper character in 'epic' activity, He can, from His all-powerful position, *allow* an epic action (that is, an action resembling the action in the classical epics), inadequate as it is, for the purpose of instructing lesser beings. The epic action has God as its director; the Christian God allows a classical plot. The God who does this is the *real* God Christians worship. Yet, if God allows an epic about Heaven itself, He must also play a part in it. This is the second role of Milton's God, a role in its proper sense, a part that he plays, reducing Himself to do so. This view not only may reconcile us to the God we see so often in the poem, but may it not also justify the whole poem in the eyes of a mystical or philosophical Christian, for his God allows the poem, even acts a part in it, but stands behind it at a sufficient distance to preserve his metaphysical divinity.

We might develop this perspective in the poem by observing Milton's God in his theological role. We find him 'permitting' several important actions. He allows Satan to leave the burning lake:

> So strecht out huge in length the Arch-fiend lay
> Chain'd on the burning Lake, nor ever thence
> Had ris'n or heav'd his head, but that the will
> And high permission of all-ruling Heaven
> Left him at large to his own dark designs . . .
>
> (I, 209–13)

He gives enough power to the opponents outside the Garden for a show of strength and controls the war in Heaven, where the

> Eternal King Omnipotent
> From his strong hold of Heav'n high over-rul'd
> And limited thir might . . .
> (VI, 227–9)

He is particularly aloof from the latter scene:

> and now all Heav'n
> Had gone to wrack, with ruin overspred
> Had not the Almightie Father where he sits
> Shrin'd in his Sanctuarie of Heav'n secure,
> Consulting on the sum of things, foreseen
> This tumult, and permitted all . . .
> (VI, 669–74)

One objective is clearly accomplished here. These are actions that are very hard to reconcile with God's omnipotence; Milton anticipates our objections by giving us the omnipotent God's position with regard to them. But may we not carry these suggestions a step further? These are the events that make for action in the poem. If we put them all together and see that God is permitting everything that makes the poem go as an epic, is it not but a slight step to picture Him allowing the whole epic, including even those events that are not specifically placed under His tolerance?

If the challenge of the earlier reading is to be met, this, I think, is the way to do it. Those who wish to make the highest claims for the poem may stop here—with some confidence in the theoretical adequacy, at least, of this answer. Perhaps some more acute and comprehensive interpretation along these general lines might eventually silence all such criticism as has arisen here. Certainly, as stated, this is an attractive perspective in which to put the poem. There are, however, some pressing questions that occur to some readers (myself obviously among them) who may be unable to hold this view, and thus unwilling to abandon the hostile perspective. In the remainder of my discussion it will be understood that I speak for these readers, those who share the responses set forth so far. For the sake of argument I will state the case in its most severe and pressing terms.

If we can maintain the above point of view throughout our reading of the poem it will certainly make a difference in our response. Most obviously, it will quiet our discomfort in a reduction of the spiritual to the material. But this was only part of the original complaint, and not the most important part. It, in itself, is not enough to defeat a conscientious reading. A more disturbing source of complaint lies in the contradiction of effects, observed particularly in the mixing of material and spiritual. Is there any help here? We can imagine the above view justifying a poem in which the literal, surface action, presented in reduced, anthropomorphic terms, had a constant relation to an ideal world. But there is no such constant relation in *Paradise Lost*. Two worlds are present, forced on our attention, and they too often imply nonsense of each other, popping in and out, or just colliding. The material presentation is not sufficiently justified by the statement that it has a correspondence to the spiritual world; the correspondence must make sense. This is true even if we can conjure the illusion that God has permitted us to use a reduced, sensuous language—the language of the epic. We still must use the language responsibly.

A further argument against this perspective is the difficulty we have in maintaining it. We may properly question how far this perspective arises naturally, without our prior theorizing, from the poem itself. Does Milton foster and encourage this perspective in the poem, or is it something we maintain in spite of what he does? A great deal depends on our ability to visualize an immediate and a remote God in the poem. This is hard to do, for they have one name and act as one person. The remote God, in this active and separate role, is too much our own construction, and, though Milton gives us material to make Him, he gives us just as much cause to forget Him. Milton does not act as if the epic particulars were forced on him by necessity but treats them as a chief glory of his subject. He wants to make us feel as if the martial equipage has something to do with God's power:

> Go then thou Mightiest in thy Fathers Might,
> Ascend my Chariot, guide the rapid Wheeles
> That shake Heav'ns basis, bring forth all my Warr,
> My Bow and Thunder, my Almightie Arms
> Gird on, and Sword upon thy puissant Thigh . . .
>
> (VI, 710–14)

Perhaps God has consented to reveal Himself in this way, but to what end? For what kind of understanding is this an accommodation? May we not object to this estimate of our understanding?

Rather than saying that this glamourous epic personage serves the purposes of the theological deity, it might be more accurate to say that Milton puts it the other way around, and uses the metaphysical attributes to enhance the glamour of his epic character. His God puts all previous military figures in the shade for might and grandeur. But Milton's claim for superiority over the ancients in this respect is hardly fair. Of course his king and army can be grander. Given the philosophical postulates of Christianity they are bound to be grander, but to use them thus is, I take it, to subvert the whole intent of those postulates. Milton has inherited a theological conception of omnipotence that really puts Achilles or Zeus in the shade; no wonder he can sing a 'more heroic' song. But this is to use the theological conception in a way foreign to the whole spirit of that conception.

Milton takes advantage of his official Christian subject to make for his poem several claims that hardly seem legitimate once we recognize the gulf between his official concerns and his actual concerns. He gives the impression of writing one kind of poem, but often writes another kind. We may so like the idea of the kind of poem he suggests he is writing that we unwittingly transfer our approval from one to the other. Doesn't Milton give a false impression of the actual poem in the invocation to Book IX:

> Not sedulous by Nature to indite
> Warrs, hitherto the onely Argument
> Heroic deem'd, chief maistrie to dissect
> With long and tedious havoc fabl'd Knights
> In Battels feign'd; the better fortitude

Of Patience and Heroic Martyrdom
Unsung; or to describe Races and Games,
Or tilting Furniture, emblazon'd Shields,
Impreses quaint, Caparisons and Steeds;
Bases and tinsel Trappings, gorgious Knights
At Joust and Tourneament; then marshal'd Feast
Serv'd up in Hall with Sewers, and Seneshals;
The skill of Artifice or office mean,
Not that which justly gives Heroic name
To Person or to Poem.

(IX, 27–41)

Does Milton really think he is singing 'the better fortitude of Patience and Heroic Martyrdom'? Where? What space and prominence does he give to it? Yet all the while he seems to me to be inditing wars, describing races, games, tilting furniture, emblazoned shields and gorgeous knights—with this difference, however, from the poems he criticizes: *his* wars, warriors, and tilting furniture are far more grand and impressive because he is dealing with the most exalted powers conceivable by the reason.

Milton is certainly not above invoking the handy metaphysical attributes of his characters when it will further his epic purposes. He uses these attributes for plain plot business:

The Filial Power arriv'd, and sate him down
With his great Father, for he also went
Invisible, yet staid (such priviledge
Hath Omnipresence) . . .

(VII, 587–90)

The theory that the Christian God allows a classical plot, attractive as it is, would remain beyond the reach of this reader if only because of these page-to-page impressions of the Christian and epic Gods in action. We can *imagine* an anthropomorphic fable, presented acceptably as a metaphorical statement on a Christian theme, and Milton may even have intended to work for some such major effect. If he did, his over-all effect is continually sapped by a series of minor effects he seems to have found irresistible. All of our attempts at justification, indeed, seem to me subverted by

Milton's own performance, his inability to resist the tempting glamour of epic business.

From this understanding of the relation between Milton's official purposes and the actual effects he works for, one is, by the way, in a position to comment on a point of much vexed debate: the style of *Paradise Lost*. Many modern readers have complained of the style for its heavy and 'unnatural' elevation, its artificiality. C. S. Lewis answers these complaints by an appeal to the requirements of the genre: the epic is supposed to be like this. The writer of the epic tries to evoke the atmosphere of a ritual occasion. Those who object, he says, have lost their appreciation of ritual.[24] If, certainly, this complaint is based on a distaste for ritual, then Lewis has justly put these persons in their places as timebound and narrowly conditioned modern readers. But is it really a distaste for ritual itself that raises objection to the style of *Paradise Lost*? Do we complain about any style *just* as a style, without reference to subject, purpose, and theme? Style is as style does, and a 'high' style cannot be absolutely bad just for being high or ritualistic. Though the modern objectors speak of the high style as bad, or distasteful to them, they must really mean that it is inappropriately high, wrongly elevated with respect to the whole trend of the poem. We may, then, have a perfectly normal respect for ritual, but we are allowed, I gather, to object to it if it seems misapplied, if the serious manner is not matched by the serious purposes that manner is to fulfil. It betrays no narrow modern prejudice in me, for example, if I find a college fraternity or lodge initiation, with all its deadly serious mumbo jumbo, a little ridiculous considering the unsublime purpose of it all.

How can this apply to Milton? How could any treatment, any style, be too exalted for his subject, God himself? True, his official subject is the most sublime one possible, as he often tells us. The question is, can we transfer the prestige of his announced subject to his every effect throughout the poem; does our God hallow his poem and justify everything he does in it? We have a right to be suspicious here, for we have seen Milton use the traditional conception of God in unfamiliar ways. Does the weight of God's purpose stand behind every effect of superficial glamour in the poem? Does God, as it were, propose to justify the ways of Milton to man? Here is where we distinguish between what Milton tells us he is doing and what effects actually work on us as we read the poem. Though we recognize the sublimity of his official theme, and respect the moral purpose of his unofficial one, we are not therefore obliged to take that as a blanket sanction for everything the poem does. In those places, then, where the height and seriousness of Milton's purposes are for us to determine (as they are everywhere, really), we may properly criticize the style for an illegitimate seriousness and weight of manner without a corresponding seriousness in the matter. It is ritual where the true purpose, as distinct from the announced purpose, will not support ritual. Thus we baulk at the high rhetorical emphasis given to the merely grand, the plain martial glamour. This is the basis for that feeling we sometimes have, as we read, of being superior to Milton: he is taking his immediate subject, so often primitive and unworthy, far more seriously than we are willing to take it.[27]

IV

The original perspective, as far as I can see, remains materially unchanged by our attempts to find some all-embracing view. A metaphorical interpretation, narrowly or broadly applied, though sound in principle, seems no more satisfactory in the end than the other defences of Milton's procedure.

I hope that by now we have earned the right to employ our original perspective so as to say clearly what is wrong with *Paradise Lost* and, in saying this, recognize how much that 'wrongness' reflects the tension between Christian and classical traditions. First, let me summarize what conclusions that perspective has permitted and how they are developed. In the very beginning, reading the Mammon passage for all that it implied, we recognized the potential danger in treating the Christian supernatural scheme in a humanly realistic narrative. Milton does not avoid the pitfalls in such a treatment. A review of the points of greatest hazard, considering the effect on a conscientious reader, shows one failure after another. Clear failures are the gross resemblances to the epic models. Less obvious, but equally deleterious, is the general parallel to those models in spirit and approach, the martial atmosphere, the glamorous heroic business. The failure here consists, first, in a reduction of the Christian heaven, and the appeal it holds for us, to an inferior sphere and an unworthy appeal. Second, and more important, the failure consists in a confusion of meanings within the Christian scheme to which the poem gives its official allegiance. This confusion is epitomized in the figure of God the Father, which is bifurcated into irreconcilable parts, so contradictory and inconsistent that it is unimaginable. Such a division is merely symptomatic, however, of a breach that splits the whole poem. The disunity shows itself in various ways. The reader is likely to apprehend it first (and most seriously) as an irresponsible use of words and an irresponsible play for effects in individual passages. He learns that he can't really believe what Milton says or give himself up to Milton's effect in one place without that meaning and effect being undermined or destroyed by his response in another place. In other words, if he is to preserve any emotional or intellectual integrity, he cannot take Milton seriously. He learns that 'surprise' does not really mean surprise or else 'omniscience' does not mean omniscience; that God does not really mean to say 'hazard' and that Raphael does not really mean that God may become 'incenst'; that Satan's unfallen adoration cannot really be fawning, cringing, and servile; that Death doesn't really threaten Satan with death; that he can't really feel horror at Satan's sword-rattling, which he elsewhere knows to be utterly ineffectual and irrelevant; that the martial combat will not be 'dreadful' and is in no danger of destroying Heaven and Earth; that Satan and Gabriel in battle dress are not 'Fit to decide the Empire of great Heav'n . . . while expectation stood in horror'. And again and again he must forget that 'spirit' means spirit, 'God' means the Christian God, and that 'Heaven' means the Christian Heaven. Another way to describe this is to say that the statements and effects in the poem have no single, embracing context. There are, rather, separate insular contexts, each in an unresolved antagonism with the other. To respond to one we must ignore the other. In the end we just lose faith in Milton's vocabulary. The trouble is, he wants us to respond to the words in their full sense in each place, yet he doesn't want to commit himself to their full meaning. We finally give up trying to read him seriously. By 'seriously' I do not mean (I hope) in a high-powered, intellectual fashion. All I mean by 'reading seriously' is that we try to believe what he says. To do this we try to understand what he says. We attend to what the words mean because we want to understand what Milton means. But it is just by attending to what the words mean in their full and normal senses that we are thrown into confusion. I think that if this goes on long enough we become fatigued at the effort and decide, perhaps subconsciously, just to share Milton's irresponsibility toward language. Like the later Eliot, we may just shut down our perceptions and accept it all as a 'shifting phantasmagory.' The illusion of harmony that Milton works for is certainly encouraged by this state of mind.

The poem's disunity may also be profitably described from another perspective, that of the tension between classical and Christian traditions. Part of the purpose of this analysis has been to show the strength of that tension. One way of perceiving the split in the poem is to see the incompatibility of the requirements Milton set out to satisfy. One set of requirements comes from his desire to imitate certain classical literary models, or, to present his subject artfully in the accepted genre developed from those models. The other set of requirements is forced on him by the demands of his subject. They are religious, or theological, requirements. That these requirements should conflict with each other is not surprising; they come, as we know, from mutually antipathetic traditions. From our reading we are forced to conclude that one set of requirements is satisfied at the expense of the other, that there is no fruitful reconciliation of the strain between them, and that the tension is unresolved. In effect, it is this conflict that pulls the poem apart.

We have attempted to reply to this reading with certain common and promising justifications of Milton's procedure. But all our attempts to explain away the misgivings we have when we read the poem carefully are unsuccessful in the long run, just as

Milton's skill at illusion is eventually unsuccessful. The truth of the matter is that we, and Milton, are trying to cover up a defect at the very core of the poem, something best described as a defect in organic form. Isn't this contradiction of effects, the disparity between official subject and actual treatment, the fragmentation of context into mutually exclusive meanings, the lack of harmony between atmosphere and theme, isn't all this precisely what we mean by a violation of organic form? Where could we more appropriately apply Coleridge's terms? 'The organic form', said Coleridge, 'is innate. It shapes as it develops itself from within, and the fulness of its development is one and the same with the perfection of its outward form.'[25] If by developing from within we mean that tone, atmosphere, imagery, emphasis, detail, event, etc.—all the things that make up the manner of presentation—are determined by the necessities of the subject or theme, the *matter*, then *Paradise Lost* does not develop from within. Its manner of presentation is not organic to its subject. This is not more true of the crude paraphernalia of the epic, which is undeniably extraneous, than it is of the more general imitation of the heroic poem, the martial bustle and sensuous dazzle of the corporeal forms. Whether led by the unwarranted prestige of the epic in his day, by a faulty and superficial reading of the epic requirements, or by plain pride in outdoing the admired ancients in their own way, Milton imposed on his Christian subject a form it does not fit. How well the poem fits Coleridge's description of mechanical form: 'The form is mechanic when on any given material we impress a pre-determined form, not necessarily arising out of the properties of the material.'[26] We remember how *Paradise Lost* took shape in Milton's mind; isn't the germ of his difficulty apparent in the very way he approached the composition of the poem? He does not have a subject or theme for which he seeks the best expression; he decides on a form which has great prestige and attraction for him, and he casts about for a subject. In the invocation to Book IX, where he defends his poem as 'heroic', he presents his case characteristically not as fit form for Christian material, but as fit material for heroic form.

How seriously does the defect in organic form damage the

poem? This is a question of the fundamental worth of the poem, always a hard and awkward question to deal with in mere words, and who would pronounce a confident verdict on *Paradise Lost*? But our inquiry has led us inevitably to this question and it would not be fair to the convictions we (meaning the 'hostile' readers) have won so far if we did not apply them to the hard questions and see what help they can give us. We cannot avoid private conclusions, and public ones, showing their grounds, can at least be disciplined and corrected. Such an attempt is properly within the province of this study. We not only want to obtain a view of the classical-Christian tension; we want to see how this view can be used.

First we must recognize the limits within which the preceding conclusions have been formed. For one thing, we have concentrated on the epic aspects of the poem, and these do not represent the whole poem. Further, even within our special interest, the emphasis may have been misleading; we may have given the impression that the epic matters are *always* set against the Christian. This is not true. We have said nothing of the harmony between the two at the ethical level, i.e. the way the epic action enforces a Christian moral. We have not mentioned Adam's actions, their consequences, and their meaning for us. In attending to the incongruities in *Paradise Lost* we have ignored all those things that are so congruent to our Christian belief: its ethical lesson, its dramatization of man's moral decisions in a great universal scheme that gives them such importance. Because of the harmony here we can't help wanting very much to become reconciled to the incongruities. Doesn't the poem do well enough for Christianity, so well that we need not be finicky about its transgressions?

If Adam is the centre of interest, then in the earlier complaint we have really been talking about the background of the poem. This background, the action in Heaven and Hell, provides the context for Adam's behaviour (and, through Adam, of all human behaviour on Earth). The whole effect of the poem, I take it, is the raising of man's decisions on Earth, his free choices, to an intense moral and teleological significance by placing them dramatically in such a great cosmological context. The reader is led to contemplate human action made crucial beyond mere human measure, each earthly decision elevated to a crisis in which the whole universe is concerned. Man's everyday choices between good and bad, operating in a great hierarchial order and seen as part of an immense cosmic struggle, take from this context a symbolic and dramatic urgency that transcends mundane vision and makes goodness matter in the nature of things. It is hard to imagine a more powerful support for moral action than this central Christian fable that Milton dramatizes. If this is the moral function of imaginative art, to bring a moral issue out of the flux of life that custom views, to dramatize the values so laid bare and make them urgent, and to lead the reader to contemplate intensely, even anxiously, the crisis so realized, then *Paradise Lost* is truly, in its design, one of the noblest attempts ever made to make moral values compelling to the imagination. Considering this design we can only regret that the poem invites and encourages the corrosive reactions that have been explored in the foregoing analysis. Yet, we cannot deny those reactions. Our proper course is to face them and ask what influence they have on the primary effect the poem seeks and how much our analysis of them permits a comment on that effect.

We have said that the perspective developed in the preceding pages views only the background of the poem, the context for Adam's behaviour. From the considerations in the above paragraph it appears that the moral force of the poem depends on the relation between this context, or background, and Adam's actions. Since our previous discussion has treated this background, presumably our conclusions have a legitimate bearing on the crucial relation between it and Adam's, or man's, moral actions. In this connection then, we are permitted to comment on the total effect of the poem.

We have seen how the background appears to a reader who tries to hold it together in his mind. At the worst it appears as a muddle of inconsistent, incongruous, and unworthy effects, full of extraneous and specious appeals, not cosmologically awesome, only dazzling. At best it is not consistently imaginable, disorganized and split, mainly because Milton is at cross purposes with himself when he treats it. Such a state of affairs would not, perhaps, force itself on our attention if Milton were not committed to use this background for purposes that demand something different, and better—if, say, the background were merely incidental, a backdrop for warrior adventures, or just plain fantasy. But Milton depends on this background for his central artistic and moral effect. He cannot afford confusion here.

If we wanted to use philosophical language to describe the confusion we could say that the imaginative world Milton evokes in *Paradise Lost* lacks a metaphysical ground, and insofar as the ethical system so fetchingly dramatized is based on some idea of ultimate reality, the metaphysical foundation, then that system is poorly supported. How can we justify a way of behaving in the world, if we don't know what kind of world it is, or can scorn the kind of world most often described to us as primitive and unworthy of the ethical vision we love? It is even more intolerable when the spiritual foundation that properly and traditionally supports that ethical vision is itself violated and abused in the process. Though the poem is ethically congruent to Christian belief, then, the trouble begins at another level, the metaphysical or, merely, the philosophical. I say it begins there because it seems very hard to prevent an infection at that level from spreading into the ethical basis of the work. If we feel this grand background for the ethical doctrine to be sham or unsound in its grandeur, can we, if this is its support, have the same respect for the ethical doctrine? If we cannot credit or even conceive such a background then we cannot fully respond, with any integrity, to the urgent drama that would lure our concern and involve our allegiance. If we can't do this, then the great design of the poem is undone. The defect in organic form is serious, not superficial, for it serves to defeat the final effect toward which the poem works.

We know that *Paradise Lost* is loved and has been loved for a long time; there is no doubt that it will be loved in the future. The analysis of the poem's defects here, certainly, is not intended to argue anyone out of a love for the poem, or to deny that the super-added attractions that hurt the poem are in their way delightful, or to minimize the tremendous achievement of the verse in individual passages, or to discourage the reading of the poem for the good it may do via the great fable it dramatizes—a mythic vessel that is powerful enough to convey its wisdom even under great handicaps. Our question is, rather, what kind of love is proper to the poem? We may properly want to make any love an examined love. And, though we may be free to admire the poem for the qualities mentioned above, we are not equally free in the claims we can make for it—as a work of art or even as a universally effective moral work. It is to these claims that this analysis does apply; any derogation of the work is offered as an effort to adjust those claims to what can be realistically admitted in a reading of the poem.

In the light of this analysis, then, how are we at last to regard the poem? Suppose one who has loved the poem comes to us with the question, 'What harm is there in asking for a reading that sees a good lesson enforced by an agreeable and exciting plot—without boring into the plot too hard?' It would be awfully stiff to say there is 'harm' in such a reading. It would be better to take from this reader a cue as to the proper place of the poem in our affections. He has asked that we read the poem as a children's poem. Isn't this what we do when we are trying to instruct children in morality: dramatize the morality in an attractive setting, or fable, even if the conditions of that setting have only a specious relation to the moral scheme? This fits *Paradise Lost*, and it may be the best way to regard the poem and its popularity after all. We should love it as we love a children's poem. Isn't *Paradise Lost*, with its gulf between the official ethical lesson and the actual ethical atmosphere, really the greatest children's poem ever written? Of course this is a fancy, but it provides a useful analogy. The comparison is worth making, if no one will misunderstand what I mean by 'children's poem' here. Through it we may become reconciled to the poem seen in proper and defensible proportion, adjusting the claims we make for it accordingly, while at the same time we face up to the point we have been forced to make all along: an adult can't read *Paradise Lost* seriously. It is the kind of poem that, if they can read it, appeals to children—or to the childlike quality in great scholars. This is not a mean or unworthy appeal. But we must take care not to make the highest claim for it; there are things very important to us that we perhaps ought not to commit to its hands—the Christian ethical and spiritual vision, for example —and we might want to establish our insights into these things on firmer grounds, firmer artistically and morally. If we make great claims for *Paradise Lost*, and let it stand for what poetry can do, and if at the same time we intend to make serious claims for poetry in competition with the claims of science, then we ought also to realize how we play into the hands of those who would see poetry as, at best, an emotive sugarcoating on the pill of doctrine. A man of science may be justified in scorning the imagination if this is its greatest work. Of course, if it turns out that we are all really children, then the joke is on our adult pretensions here, and Milton's praise is restored in the very phrase that seems to take it away.

NOTES TO CHAPTER V

[1] See p. 90.

[2] Citations from Milton in my text are to *The Works of John Milton* (New York, 1931–9), the Columbia Milton.

[3] See Caroline Mayerson, 'The Orpheus Image in *Lycidas*', *PMLA*, LXIV (1949), 189–207.

[4] *Milton* (London, 1900), p. 255.

[5] *Ibid.*, p. 85.

[6] *The Seventeenth Century Background* (London, 1934), p. 232f.

[7] *L'Art Poetique*, III, 193–204.

[8] 'Milton', *The Lives of the English Poets* (London: Everyman's Library, 1925), I, 96.

[9] Andrew Marvell, *Poems and Letters*, ed. H. M. Margoliouth (Oxford, 1927), I, 131.

[10] *Lives of the English Poets*, pp. 108–9.

[11] 'Milton', *Edinburgh Review*, August, 1825.

[12] *Paradise Lost in Our Time* (New York, 1948), p. 59. One of the most acute commentaries on this difficulty appears in A. J. A. Waldock's *Paradise Lost and its Critics* (Cambridge, England, 1947), chapter V. Though my views often parallel Waldock's I have chosen to make my case from my own beginnings despite the risk of repetition.

[13] It may be objected here, and later, that none of these associations are, in fact, evoked in the passages I cite. Any reader may claim that there are no such associations *for him*, and that therefore any argument based on this 'evidence' is worthless. I agree that if a reader does not share what I think to be the normal and common reaction here, and elsewhere, then the rest of my argument will lead to no useful conclusion for him. I know of no way to convince such a reader. It is impossible to *prove* connotations; we merely hold them up for each other to see, as it were, and then, if we intend to make a critical point, go on to show the implications of those connotations to those who share our reaction. The rest, who cannot be privileged to object at random, must make coherent sense from their own beginnings. It seems fruitless to argue the original response; time and the norm of reader sensibility will settle the question, I take it, and we look there for corroboration—which is all we hope for in such a matter, rather than argued proof. On the other hand, even for those who feel that the reactions I display are private (and any critic must admit fallibility here) the succeeding argument may still be of some worth. It becomes then merely the carrying out of an if-then proposition: if this is the quality of each passage examined then the consequences for the whole poem are thus and so. This is the proposition that can be fruitfully argued; it is public and debatable, open to rational correction. I would be content here to obtain agreement on it alone—and submit the rest to the corroborating sensibility of the reader. I am not so confident of my instinct for suggestions and associations that I would claim the same kind of validity for it.

[14] I do not here mean to enter the great debate over the nature of an epic, nor even to make any confident claims for what Milton took to be the nature of the epic. Much less do I wish to imply by my phrase 'requirement of the epic' that there exists a rigid set of specifications in Milton's, or anybody's, mind when he sets out to write an epic. What Milton *thinks* is an epic, and what it requires, is what really matters here, but this is very difficult to know clearly. What we do know is that these things get into his poem, and the most reasonable explanation is that they spring from some general desire by the poet to write an epic-like poem. We know the general characteristics of his epic models; these things are in them. If Milton wants to rival his models, as he says he does, then such qualities apparently act as general 'requirements' he is trying to meet. What other motive or source is responsible for them? That is all I mean by 'requirement of the epic.'

[15] *Lives of the English Poets*, I, 109.

[16] Introduction to *The English Poems of John Milton* (London: The World's Classics, 1940); commonly available in the United States in *Milton Criticism*, ed. James Thorpe (New York, 1950), pp. 252–66.

[17] (Oxford, 1942), chapters IV, VII, VIII, *passim*.

[18] *Preface to Paradise Lost*, p. 105. The rest of Lewis's argument summarized below appears on pp. 105–8.

[19] From the Henriette Hertz Lecture, delivered to the British Academy, March 26, 1947. Commonly available in *T. S. Eliot. Selected Prose*, ed. John Hayward (London: Penguin Books, 1953), from which this is taken, p. 144.

[20] Students of recent Milton controversy will recognize this as a main point of Lewis's *Preface to Paradise Lost*, where it is lucidly and eloquently argued. I would prefer to present these common defences as possible and reasonable positions, without singling out spokesmen for special responsibility. Lewis, however, is so persuasive that his name must inevitably stand for the defence.

[21] 'The War in Heaven', *Answerable Style* (Minneapolis, 1953), pp. 17–37.

[22] *Ibid.*, p. 17.

[23] See *De Doctrina Christiana*, chapter II.

[24] See *Preface to PL*, chapters I, III, IV, VII, VIII.

[25] *Coleridge's Shakespearean Criticism*, ed. Thomas M. Raysor (Cambridge, Mass., 1930), I, 224.

[26] *Loc. cit.*

[27] I am sorry to say that John D. Peter's important book, *A Critique of Paradise Lost* (London, 1960), came to my attention too late for me to make use of it in this essay. Awareness of his 'corroborating sensibility' would have braced (and shortened) my comments on several passages.

CHAPTER VI

Conclusion

THOUGH THE primary purpose of these essays has been to exhibit the critical usefulness of a perspective, and not to assemble data for historical generalizations, yet enough information has been accumulated to invite some evaluation of the evidence in general terms. First of all, if we did not know it already, the review of these four poets supports the conclusion that the classical-Christian conflict is an issue worth keeping in mind as we read seventeenth-century poetry. More than this, we may draw from the evidence reviewed in the foregoing pages some insight into the question of how this conflict, or tension, is involved in the general make-up of the poetry as a whole, how it relates to those distinguishing characteristics of seventeenth-century poetry that readers have found valuable and how far it provides useful terms for talking about those characteristics. A peak of poetic achievement, particularly in the lyric, is generally recognized in the period and, inasmuch as the conflict between traditions reaches some kind of climax here, we might naturally consider this a good place to assess its general operation in the poetry.

With respect to the erotic lyric, using the poetry of Robert Herrick, we have seen that the tension, however it operates in the psychology of the poet, functions in the poetry to produce a particular complexity and depth. This kind of complexity is not present in the line of carnal poetry developed exclusively in the classical tradition, poetry revealing no consciousness of a Christian viewpoint. If we want to use the tension as a standard by which to discriminate among various poets, or periods, we can see how this distinguishes Herrick from, say, the Elizabethan courtly poets, or the 'pure' classicist Ben Jonson, or the uniformly pagan Cavaliers such as Suckling or Lovelace.

The heightened conflict of classical and Christian traditions may make for this complexity, apparently, in that it forces an awareness of competing values. When this happens to the right sensibility, the conflict results in what is properly called 'tension' in its strict sense, an opposition without destructive negation. It is a mode of perception that makes use of values 'on the other side', even if the usefulness be only that of the anvil on which one's determined views are hammered out. In Herrick's most admired poems (*Corinna*, for example) the values of one kind of experience are realized and defined against the opposition or resistance of another kind. We call these poems 'complex' not because they are tortured and difficult but because of the multiple or intricate values they recognize and, in a way, reconcile. In them we have a perspective that allows us to perceive the value of one order of experience without denying the claims of another order. What historical conditions favour this we can't say dogmatically, but certainly such a perspective would be nourished by a milieu in which each side of the conflict was continually set forth in its most pressing terms and conceived in its most vivid imagery. Of course it is the particular poet, whose sensibility reacts to these pressures, that transforms the conflict into a fruitful tension.

An even greater complexity is apparent in the poetry of Andrew Marvell, who plays the two traditions against each other in a way that places him in neither one, yet which shows him highly conscious of values and limitations in both. We have observed how much his conception of nature, his 'pastoralism', is in debt to each tradition, and how at the same time it provides him a 'third position' which allows him a critical view of those traditions too. In his poetry the tension serves as the generating force for a whole set of opposed images and attitudes; his characteristic complexity seems, therefore, to owe a great deal to the conflict of traditions. What distinguishes Marvell's poetry particularly from that of other poets who merely *express* the conflict, weighted to one side or the other, is his ability to maintain the tension, to an even greater extent than Herrick, in a fruitful and ordered balance that opposes but does not overwhelm values on each side of the scale.

In the religious lyric we observed a different but related problem. There the Christian poet is faced with the paradoxical requirement that devotional poetry should not really be poetry, i.e. the devices of the imagination are not supposed to be necessary or proper to real devotion; yet, on the other hand, it is an abomination to find all the efforts of the imagination turned only to sensual uses. One way out, the severely Christian way, is to write only the simple hymn of prayer and praise, the uncomplicated hosanna, or the unreserved contempt of the world. In its adherence to a single tradition, and in its lack of tension, this corresponds to the single-minded erotic lyric. It is not what we get in George Herbert, though it is what he continually praises, for in Herbert, paralleling what we find in Herrick in the erotic lyric, the tension is associated with a complexity and depth not like anything in the holy line of poetry developed exclusively in the Christian tradition, i.e. the tradition that shuns the strategies of the literary tradition. For Herbert, guilty as he felt about it, employs a language of devotion that takes full advantage of all the devices of the imagination, making fullest use of the strategies developed in the literary tradition. Yet all this is for the purpose of dramatizing and heightening the simple devotional affirmation his religious feeling required, defining the value of that affirmation in the embattled human context that only the full poetic setting can bring to life. Paradoxically, Herbert must use artifice to show the context in which the simple, heart-felt affirmation (which denies artifice) has its meaning and value. True devotion is simple and direct, but the language that does justice to devotion in its human setting is complex. Herbert's best religious poems are no more the pure paeans of praise and worship than Herrick's best mirth poems are pure paeans of carnal joy.

In the poetry of all three of these poets the common feature with which we associate the tension is complexity, a sophistication in perspective. When we talk about this complexity, the terms developed through a view of the conflict of traditions are particularly useful. They may, for one thing, help us understand why this kind of complexity may be so admired—as it has been in modern times. At least we can see cause why this poetry might have a

special attraction beyond that of the uncomplicated erotic or religious lyric exhibiting no consciousness of the opposing tradition.
For if the Christian, with its cluster of images and associations, and
the pagan, with its cluster, actually happen to represent certain
everpresent values in human life, neither one of them a self-suffi-
cient good, then this poetry would seem to offer a very mature
and realistic perspective on them. The point of greatest insight
would lie not in a complete commitment to either (i.e. one so
strong that it excludes consciousness of the other) but in an awareness of the values in opposition. In this case, each side represents a
pull that should always be felt, but which should never completely
overpower its opposition. We should be careful not to regard this
as some kind of golden mean, or even as a harmonious 'synthesis'.
We cannot call it simply a 'reconciliation' of opposites, for the
value at one side may be most acutely defined and realized because
it is set *against* the other; the conflict or tension may operate best
when it is most rigorously maintained. The complex consciousness fostered here need not exclude allegiances; it may merely
make them more wise, or more poignant. Herrick does not sacrifice his sensuality to some middle ground, nor does Herbert dilute
his devotion. The intensified conflict, the compelling attraction of
both rival values, may heighten and define the worth of each. It
may then be no accident that the love lyric and the religious lyric
simultaneously reach their greatest glory here in the seventeenth
century.

For an evaluation of the critical perspective employed here,
as distinct from the above evaluation of the plain information
assembled, we can only refer to the worth for the reader of the
individual analyses in the essays treating the three poets. I hope it
has been shown there that this is a useful approach to many very
interesting poems. No one would claim that an approach like this
is exhaustively explanatory. In the work of each poet we find a
great mass of poems we can't talk about profitably in connection
with the classical-Christian conflict, but the poems we do take,
though few in number, are for the most part good poems,
characteristic of the poet, and distinctive of the age. And we have
no reason to believe that the habit of mind and sensibility found

working obviously in these poems is not at work more subtly in a great many others. Yet the matter is not so obvious that a guided reading and criticism is unnecessary, that there is no need to train our eyesight with scholarship in the accurate construction of a historical perspective. This sort of aid to the reader particularly requires, and justifies, an academic service.

The resulting study of these three poets, though the emphasis has varied from one to the other, exhibits an obvious unity. Milton seems to present a different problem. We know his work is relevant to a study of the classical-Christian conflict when we consider his mingling of the traditions, his obvious consciousness of the conflict, and his Christian uneasiness at times in the use of classical reference. In at least one work, *Lycidas*, he may come closer to a harmonious fusion of the two traditions than any other poet. But, in view of the fundamental problem in *Paradise Lost*, these have here been regarded as secondary issues. The problem treated in *Paradise Lost* may seem to take us into an entirely different branch of the classical-Christian conflict. At least the clash of traditions appears in that poem in a different form.

Yet the difference is not so great as it would first seem. What is it that gives Milton trouble in *Paradise Lost*? It is the philosophical and mystical abstraction, the otherworldly strain in the Christian religion. It means potential trouble for any poetry for it resists physical, realistic embodiment; it cannot readily take a part in an immediate and particular human context. Some religious poetry seems to give place to these ineffabilities, but the real subject of such poetry is usually, on second look, more accurately seen to be the worshipper's experience of and attitude toward God. His situation is made personally dramatic; the place of God in this context is seen indirectly through the speaker. The immediate business of the poem is a concrete, particular, human context. This is what Herbert's religious poems are like, and Donne's too. The poet, because of God's metaphysical ineffability, cannot describe Him directly, as Donne recognizes:

> Eternal God (for whom who ever dare
> Seek new expressions, doe the Circle square,

And thrust into strait corners of poore wit
Thee, who art cornerlesse and infinite)
I would but blesse thy name, not name thee now.[1]

The art of poetry does what is proper to it; it makes the human context come alive to us. Yet the concrete particularities of poetry are, from the point of view of the philosophical abstraction, always inferior, for the *real* world is of the spirit. Herbert regretted that the conveying of God's presence required this intermediary artifice, but he made it serve him successfully. And Herbert's discomfort is small compared to those Christian poets who, in addition, deal with profane subjects, with the world and the flesh, which are not only inferior but positively bad. Milton, however, makes a frontal attack. He proposes to put God himself into the worldly human context of a narrative poem—and not as a myth, but as a literal truth. There all the forces that make for a Christian conflict with 'worldly' poetry work within the very poem itself to undermine and disorganize it. Thus we see that the tension, which may serve constructively to define values in certain contexts, can also be destructive. If Milton's religious purpose is confounded it is because he tries to 'thrust into strait corners of poore wit' a God who is 'cornerlesse and infinite.'

The true religion does not become fiction so well as a false, as Sir William Temple noted,[2] partly because we have no choice, with this conception of the true God, but to be in complete earnest about the religious aspect of the poem; we can't just relax and enjoy the story. When Milton takes the subject he does he asks, as he does in other ways, for a solemn and earnest religious reading. But, for the enjoyment of the poem, i.e. of the fine 'human' narrative, that is the wrong way to read it. We tried it that way and the result is too solemn, too serious for the good human poem that is there to be enjoyed. Even *Paradise Lost*, the best poem of its kind, when given the serious reading the poet requests and the subject demands, seems rather 'to debase religion than to heighten poetry.'

Many interesting questions must remain here imperfectly answered, or even unasked. There are deeper implications of the classical-Christian conflict that we have hardly begun to explore, considerations that invite a much more philosophical and theoretical treatment. If we were to generalize on the long history of Christian suspicion and complaint, looking for the denominator in the views that give poetry the most trouble, we might find that, from poetry's point of view, the final villain of the whole piece is the abstraction, the faith that a superior sort of reality is found in the *idea*, and that the Christian resistance to poetry is one version of a much more general view that is inherently hostile to poetry—at least to poetry as an imaginative art rather than a vehicle for doctrine or ideas. It would be convenient to fasten the whole blame on Plato. Certainly we can see that it is the contribution of Greek speculative thought, the otherworldly Platonic strain that gets into Christianity, that accounts for a great deal of the resistance to poetry.

Yet we would not want to limit a description of the view that discredits poetry just to an otherworldly philosophy. The broader habit of mind behind this opposition is, essentially, one which would limit truth to the abstraction, and this may take in other philosophies, including certain scientific habits of mind. Science as a structure of mathematically ordered abstracta from direct experience may substitute an abstraction that acquires the same 'truth' prestige as the Platonic Idea; the prestige is less mystical but it discredits the fictions of poetry in the same way. Seen in this light, poetry in the seventeenth century faces fundamentally the same challenge from both religion and the new science. It is surprising how much some of the scientific complaints against poetry sound like the characteristic Christian complaints. Basil Willey cites, for example, a complaint by Thomas Sprat in his *History of the Royal Society* against classical machinery that could, we sense, be placed without change directly into the mouth of a Puritan assailing the classical literary tradition:

The Wit of the Fables and Religions of the Antient World, is well-nigh consum'd: They have already serv'd the poets long enough; and it is now high time to dismiss them; especially seeing they have this peculiar imperfection, that they were only Fictions at first: whereas Truth is never so well express'd or amplify'd, as by those Ornaments which are True and Real in themselves.[3]

From this point of view the so-called 'dissociation of sensibility', the split between thought and feeling found by T. S. Eliot to take place after the seventeenth century, is a divisive tendency latent in Western culture from the beginning and operative in poetry, through one kind of Christian influence, for a very long time. It is significant that this divisive tendency should be felt most strongly in the seventeenth century, a period for which unity of sensibility in the poetry is usually claimed. This claim, as Leonard Unger points out, mistakes a yearning for unity for unity itself:

> There was no unique fusion in the poetry, and there was no utter unity in the poets. The unity, like the fusion, has been an effect of seventeenth-century poetry on modern readers, and not a condition of the seventeenth-century poets. I suggest that the poetry of Donne and Marvell reflects not a pre-existing unity in the poets, but rather an urgent search for unity by the poets.[4]

Also of interest is the historical question: Why does the classical-Christian conflict come to a climax in the seventeenth century? It seems that the literary and religious spheres could be kept separate fairly well in the early Renaissance period and the Christian poet could don the mask of Ovid fairly easily. Poetry was a 'let's pretend' literary game compartmented rather securely from the poet's personal religious beliefs. Do we have the inevitable but gradual recognition of the implications of this game, a kind of cultural lag? Or can we account for it by the fact that the surge of Puritan spirit reaches its height in this period, this phenomenon coming at the same time that poets mastered and realized the full possibilities of the Renaissance literary forms developed under classical impetus? Does this give us any insight into those large but handy formulas for the age—such as the description of the seventeenth century as the period in which the spirit of the Reformation combats the spirit of the Renaissance? The speculation is certainly given point by those who, like C. M. Bowra, find in the personality of Milton a tension between the Puritan and the Humanist.[5]

Similar to this question is another one. What happens to the classical-Christian conflict after this? Why does the conflict cool at the end of the seventeenth century and become cold in the eighteenth? Looking only at the surface of the matter, the intensity of feeling attached to each kind of reference seems to subside quite rapidly. Certainly Augustan classicism makes small use of the 'paganism' in classical reference. An exact formulation of these loose questions and suggestive fancies might well be worthwhile. It is not really new evidence that we look for here, not research, as if the classical-Christian conflict were a new subject, but a review of evidence already formulated in other terms. The classical-Christian conflict merely provides a perspective, a set of binoculars with a particular focus, which, systematically used, may reveal old issues in a familiar but usefully organized scene. At least that is what has been attempted here.

NOTES TO CHAPTER VI

[1] *John Donne: Complete Poetry and Selected Prose*, ed. John Hayward (Bloomsbury, 1929), p. 302.
[2] See p. 37.
[3] *The Seventeenth Century Background* (London, 1934), p. 216.
[4] Leonard Unger, *The Man in the Name* (Minneapolis, 1956), p. 123.
[5] See C. M. Bowra, *From Virgil to Milton* (London, 1945), pp. 243ff.

Index